STRICTLY POSITIVE TEACHING

BY
FRANCES COX

How positive classroom practice can improve behaviour management, help learners learn better, and make students and their teachers happier and healthier

CONTENTS

Preface 1

WHY STRICTLY POSITIVE TEACHING? THE POSITIVE REASONS

The *Oxford English Dictionary* defines positivity as "the practice of being or tendency to be positive or optimistic in attitude". Interestingly, the illustration of the word is "pupils draw power from the positivity of their teachers".

The difference between positivity and optimism, however, is that to be optimistic you need only hope and believe that things will be good, whereas positivity implies a level of work to improve the chances of a good outcome.

Positivity gets a bad press. It sometimes seems as if it's uncool to be upbeat and positive in workplaces where the prevailing mood is gloom, and while the popular stereotype of the moaning teacher is just that – a stereotype – that doesn't mean examples of the type don't exist. There is a tendency to see positivity as naivety and a more cynical attitude to the world, generally looking for proof that it's not a great place and one you can make wry cracks about, is much more reassuring. Perhaps the explanation is that if you paint your world as less than brilliant, and the chances of changing it virtually nil, then you can't be unpleasantly surprised when things go wrong, or when your efforts fail to bring about significant change for the better. It was always bound to be that way because things are inherently not great. Nothing to do with me, mate. Just the way things are. A less-than-positive outlook can, according to those people who adopt it, act as a shield against things going wrong.

I would suggest to everybody, however, that it is time to be brave. Step up to the present and the future and accept that you can, through a small shift in your outlook, make some things better with a positive attitude.

Indeed, research shows that in many areas having a positive attitude has surprising benefits. Researchers continue to look into the effects of positive thinking and optimism on health and well-being, and it appears there are few areas in which positive individuals cannot derive advantages. They tend to live healthier lifestyles, perhaps because they look forward to a long life. They have increased life-span, lower rates of depression and distress and consequent better psychological well-being, better coping skills during times of hardship and stress and therefore better resilience. Physically they have better cardiovascular health and are less likely to die from cardiovascular disease. They are even less susceptible to the common cold.

All of which is very desirable and particularly important for everyone living in these "interesting times", but especially important for young people and those who are charged with educating them.

Preface 2

WHY STRICTLY POSITIVE TEACHING? THE NEGATIVE REASONS

I am aware this is an ironic element to include in a book where the title (and every chapter) refers to remaining "Strictly Positive", but it is important to understand the background to the educational world we live in today and the factors that make positive attitudes in school incredibly important.

What follows is, I promise, the only resolutely downbeat five pages of this book. I apologise for that, but at the core of the Strictly Positive Teaching philosophy is an awareness of factors which combine against good mental health in schools, among teachers as well as among young people of school age. For that reason, I think it is worth briefly examining where we are right now and what, therefore, becomes our starting point.

It's a very tough time to be a child. It's not that easy for the rest of us, but it doesn't take much of a stretch of imagination to see that it must be unbelievably scary and confusing through the lens of a child.

We have lived through a globally tumultuous few years, where much of what we took for granted has been thrown out of the window. In the western world populations have never been so divided since the days of the Cold War. Within nations the holders of entrenched views seem unable to understand the opposing opinion. Anger and contempt greet any expression of views from the other side.

In the international English-speaking world, we are now living in a "post-truth" era. The phrase "fake news", unknown a couple of years ago, is an explicit concept which people now accept. Cries of "fake news" are chorused by one side when a report seems to claim that their opinions might be misguided. Individuals trust their own prejudices more than facts or the opinions of experts. "Expert" has become a pejorative term, as people grasp the opportunity to assert their own opinions, however misguided and extreme they may be. Norms have been overturned with the controversial election of Donald Trump in the USA, and Brexit in the UK. Our leaders blithely lie and dissemble, and shy away from detail. When they are caught out in lies and dissimulation they show no shame, but tough it out, make outrageous excuses and lie some more. In both nations divisions have not been thrown into such sharp focus for many decades. As the dust settles, even so many months after the events, the deep fault lines of disagreement endure. One man's facts are another man's "fake news". Lies, or "alternative facts", are everywhere.

Migration is another hot topic everywhere; while unfortunates flee strife, war, famine and poverty from many nations of the earth, and liberals across the globe reason that whole-world problems require whole-world solutions, impoverished communities in the developed world believe they pay a disproportionate price in helping the poor and exiled of the globe, and they seek to pull up the drawbridges and concentrate on looking after their own. Migrants living here, Europeans as well as those from further away, are looked at with a more open distrust, and in Britain and America instances of hate crime have surged since our two elections, at some point more than doubling compared to the days before the two surprise results. Some schools have started collecting ethnic data about their students. Individuals are disappearing from communities where they have lived for decades. Hate crimes are rising and racism and bigotry seem to grow unchecked. Children are fearful.

Economically the western world continues to feel the impact of a massive economic crisis and uncertainty, so that families are anxiously watching their budgets and fearing the economic ramifications of these seismic political events. Many Britons live in deep poverty, having to judge what bills not to pay, and rely on food banks, in some cases turning to the frankly terrifying resort of loan sharks. Children living in such circumstances feel helpless and frightened, sometimes experiencing anxiety and guilt that they are unable to help their families.

In the UK schools are often congratulated by the Office for Standards in Education (Ofsted) on their "relentless drive for improvement", "relentless commitment", and "relentless hard work" when their performance is judged to have improved. Relentless is a tough word to tolerate when it pertains to people working with young people, people who rely on those young people for that improvement. Judgements of a school's performance may look at "pupils' spiritual, moral, social and cultural development" and their "personal development, behaviour and welfare" but, whatever the facts, most schools interpret the overwhelming priority as enabling students to get the highest grades in SATs, GCSEs, A Levels, etc that they can.

Recent utterances from Ofsted indicate this may change, and it is profoundly to be hoped that it will. It will be a brave school that leads the way and takes them at their word, though... Of course, it is the core business of a school to get their students the best possible qualifications so they can walk out of the doors into the best future they can build for themselves. The obvious danger, however, is that if those grades mean more to the school than to the students, any incidental detriment to the student in the attempt to get them can be easily overlooked. In addition, the value of arts education is being questioned by authorities anxious to provide students with skills that will fit them for the demands of the modern workplace. Some people accept without argument the idea that the function of school is to provide workers. Education for its own sake is not a popular cause – but it is hard to argue that inculcating and nurturing a love of the arts, of music, of sports, of philosophy in the sense of thinking complex, abstract thoughts, is not important to the formation of a whole, rounded, healthy person.

Social media is often a forum for hate, loathing and dismissal; children who are subjected to bullying are not safe when they close their bedroom doors, but are followed in and tormented mercilessly through their electronic devices. The bully in the playground and behind the bike-sheds has been replaced by the faceless bullies ranged at thousands of keyboards tapping out insidious and unrelenting abuse. Children in friendships and relationships routinely exchange photos of themselves naked or semi-naked for a laugh, and then when relationships go wrong those intimate photos can be widely exchanged and judged cruelly and obscenely. "Revenge porn" is a thing. And if public figures are regularly subjected to rape and death threats, can we be surprised that some young people choose to mete out the same to other, more vulnerable, youngsters? We are becoming desensitised to the pictures of children and young people who have committed suicide staring out at us from the front pages of our newspapers.

As I said, it's a tough old world. Stress, depression and anxiety are therefore as endemic in schools as they are in the wider population.

This epidemic of mental health issues is widely acknowledged by politicians and those in power, but it would be too daunting to try to address the root causes – impossible, even. So Theresa May announces that the "stigma" of mental health issues must be tackled, but declines to provide any funding to do so... instead, predictably, saying that schools and employers will provide this support for children. The government may recognise the rising tide of mental health issues among our young, which threatens to engulf our schools, but the only response is that well-being and meditation classes will be provided in some schools, and individuals already working in schools will be trained to counsel young people – a half-hearted response at best and, at worst, dangerous in that it tries to help solve complex problems with a little knowledge. No one seems to question the fact that our young people are suffering and cutting themselves and killing themselves, and the system might be in part to blame. The government seeks ways to manage these issues rather than eliminate, or at least mitigate, the circumstances which bring them about.

A 2018 Dutch report describes a world where one in five teachers experiences burnout symptoms, where teachers' workloads often exceed those of other professionals and where teachers new to the profession are especially likely to suffer stress. They show that such pressures on teachers are actually detrimental to the level of their students' achievements – ironic, when we consider that the stress heaped on teachers by themselves and their leadership teams is all in the name of raising their students' life chances.

We in schools are used to governments calling upon us to resolve all the issues which beset society without any money, training or time – in addition to teaching and helping students get good grades. We sigh, moan a bit, then roll up our sleeves and get on with it.

But the truth is, in this area, we teachers *can* do something to help. We can do something to help in our everyday pedagogical practice. We should not aim to be ersatz psychiatrists or social workers – as teachers we are not qualified to replace such professionals, and trying ham-fistedly to do so could do more harm than good; even school pastoral leaders cannot do any more than acknowledge concerns about a student and signpost or access appropriate sources of help. But in our classrooms and in our schools, we *can* help.

As a stark contrast to all the insoluble awfulness of the world, we can resolve to be kind, strict and *positive*. Kind, because we recognise the stresses and strains which young people and teachers are subjected to; strict, because there is nothing more confusing and unsettling for a young person than inconsistency and shifting boundaries; and positive because it is important for a young person to know their teachers are interested in the good they do, their genuine achievements and the real efforts they make, not just their mistakes and omissions.

In every aspect of our work as teachers we can resolve to provide clear boundaries to the students in our care while being unfailingly positive. We can work with the natural psychology of being a child, rather than forcing young people to behave in ways that run counter to their instincts, and expecting them to fall in with our adult rhythms. In every sphere of operation we can resolve to be a *Strictly Positive Teacher*.

These are my two pages of bad news. An ironic introduction to the concept of Strictly Positive Teaching, but everything from now on will be positive.

UPDATE: since writing this preface, I have had to attend the funeral of a creative, talented young person, the same age as my son and from the same school year, who buckled under the strain of life and took his own life just a year after leaving school. My evangelical zeal for Strictly Positive Teaching has intensified.

Introduction

STRICTLY POSITIVE TEACHING

"It's just looking at things from a different perspective..."

So began my pitch to the Senior Leadership Team (SLT) when I decided I wanted the chance to roll out to the rest of our staff the behaviour-management techniques that had worked so well for me for a decade.

And as soon as the words were out of my mouth I realised it wasn't "just" anything – rather, it was a completely different way of looking at teaching, the classroom, the students, everything. As I expounded on my theories of behaviour management, and described case studies of students known to the team, where these techniques had served me well, I was slightly distracted by what my idea of Strictly Positive Teaching actually was.

It started in 1995 with a training day in which we were taught to draw two faces and put them on each side of the board: a smiley face on one side, and a sad face on the other, and then write names under them.

So far, so very, *very* ordinary. There can be few teachers who haven't seen that in their schools. (However, I would argue that many, *many*

people will have seen it done in a way that is not positive. Many people will have seen it used in a very, *very* negative way.)

But over the years Strictly Positive Teaching has grown into a cohesive philosophy which can guide and direct all aspects of a teacher's practice.

Major confession #1: I never wanted to write this book. I find writing non-fiction laborious and draining, and I find structuring my thoughts almost impossible. Sitting down to write makes me remember something else I need to do, something fascinating like cleaning the dishwasher or vacuuming. But this is a mission. I tried very hard to find a version of this book written by someone else to let me off the hook, but I failed.

I've been searching for it for a while now, buying and reading a lot of books, always hoping the next one will be the one that means I don't have to write mine. I've been reading around the subject, looking at teaching handbooks and educational theorists' blogs, articles and letters, and I haven't yet found a comprehensive exploration that puts all the different aspects of Strictly Positive Teaching together into a cohesive whole.

So that is what I am going to do here. I tried to complete this book while teaching a full timetable but, like many teachers, I've found teaching to be a job that doesn't allow for much else during term time. I couldn't combine my twelve-hour teaching day with coming home and writing, and I have a family whom I have neglected too long. I've therefore given up my teaching career because this is now my teaching vocation, my mission. I feel I can better help teachers and young people by writing this book than by simply talking to my colleagues. Strictly Positive Teaching is my mission.

This is not an academic book, although as I have read a lot of books about pedagogy and psychology I have obviously drawn from them. This is a handbook of strategies which have helped me and many others in the classroom over the years, and which I have shared with colleagues who have found them invaluable. It's a pick-and-mix approach to making your classroom and your teaching more positive. I include case studies, examples and suggestions from former colleagues from different parts of the school community and from contacts in outside agencies.

There are a few buzzwords and ideas I need to discuss first as part of the justification for the Strictly Positive approach.

❖ Happiness and well-being

"The purpose of life is to be happy." The Dalai Lama

I dislike the way the term "well-being" is used, in the same way that I dislike the way people talk of "happiness". For many years the "happiness" industry has monetised the idea of happiness, selling the impression that happiness is a state in and of itself and something you can seek to create. Most research on the subject suggests this is not true. We become happy by doing things that make us happy and give us a sense of purpose, usefulness or calm. Ed Diener, professor of psychology and a senior scientist for the Gallup organisation, has done decades of research into societies around the globe, and asserts that happiness comes from many factors, chief among which are:

- *Social relationships: friends, colleagues, spouses, family. We are social beings and need to feel we have a place*
- *Work, paid or unpaid, that we love: doing something that feels worthwhile makes you happy*
- *Active leisure: no one became happy by sitting on the sofa watching Keeping up with the Kardashians and reruns of Friends*
- *Having a positive attitude: goes without saying*
- *Using our skills: everyone likes to feel useful*
- *Constant learning: formal or informal. We don't have to go back to school*
- *Having life goals beyond ourselves: this does not include acquiring things, which emphatically doesn't make us happy*

Furthermore, a state of happiness or contentment is a continuum that extends from being clinically depressed, to deeply unhappy through satisfied and content, to wildly happy at times of extreme joy – a wedding, say, or the birth of a child. The consumer culture tells us we can become happy by spending money, by buying things or experiences, and indeed this assertion is screamed at us every moment of our day and is repeated so often and reinforced by consumerism and the advertising industry so much, that it is widely accepted as inalienable fact. Research, however, inconveniently suggests the reverse is true: that if you really want that gorgeously soft suede jacket, the one you've seen on the website of your favourite clothes business, the one that's apparently so popular that stock is running out, buying that jacket will not make you happy. You will love it, open it with pleasure, try it on and marvel at how beautiful it is and how everyone else will love it on you, and then... it will rapidly cease to be the thing which brings you pleasure... but those boots! The ankle boots, more than you would normally spend, they are the purchase that will definitely bring you so much pleasure you won't need to buy anything else for... oh, ages!

So you buy them, and guess what? You realise that what you really need is a coat, or a holiday, or a car. The cycle repeats itself *ad nauseam*. It's why children are excited about Christmas Day and then miserable when they've unwrapped all their presents. A sobering read is *Born to Buy – the Commercialized Child and the New Consumer Culture* by J B Schor, which examines the causes and consequences of the materialistic values very deliberately instilled in children by American business. And, published in 2004, this was before internet advertising, social media and apps, which make desiring and buying so addictively easy.

What actually makes people happy is other people – loving them, spending time with them, volunteering to help them, having a drink in the pub with them, having fun with them. Pets also make us happy, as does exercise, kindness, making time for culture and positive thinking. Worrying about being happy actually makes us unhappy.

William Davies' book on *The Happiness Industry* is subtitled *How the Government and Big Business sold us Well-Being*. You probably don't need any more detail than that.

Well-being has come to have similar connotations as this monetised idea of happiness. Everyone now talks about well-being as something which you pursue as a thing in itself. You can buy well-being apps for your phone, go on well-being courses, have well-being counselling, become a well-being coach. Well-being is the new happiness. In 2017 the Children and Young People's Mental Health Coalition expressed a concern about this trend, especially in the context of schools. Vice-Chair Dr Pooky Knightsmith said that placing undue trust in the benefits of meditation and mindfulness exercises could actually negatively affect the mental health of vulnerable young people with a history of trauma. An excessive emphasis on happiness above all other emotions can be damaging by suggesting that other emotions are toxic and risks pathologising feelings other than happiness and calm for all young people.

Isn't well-being the state of being well? And doesn't everything you do in life contribute to your being well or unwell? If you hate your job and you're unhappy in your marriage and are worrying about your aged parent or sick child, no app in the world is going to give you "well-being" because it can't make you be well – it can be a sticking plaster, a spiritual medicament, but it can't make you well. And that's okay. My problem is the lazy nomenclature.

Well-being surely stems from doing things that make you well. The way you live your life will help you to be well. It can't do anything about some areas of your life, and maybe that's just something we have to accept. Spending money won't change that. Reinhold Niebuhr's *Serenity Prayer* asks for "the serenity to accept the things I cannot change, the courage to change the things I can change, and the wisdom to know the difference". And for some that is where real well-being comes from. Too many sensitive people, especially the young, experience significant existential trauma because they find it difficult to face the reality of all the dreadful events happening around the world, and their perceived powerlessness to help. We need to create a society in which people can be well. Well-being comes out of doing things that make us well. Well-being doesn't come from meditating to *forget* about what's wrong in life – that's not what meditation is about – or mindfulness to focus only on the here and now and sideline anything inconvenient. They might help, but they're not the main thing.

If the powers that be really want to raise the level of well-being in schools, they need to create the conditions which make students well, and tackle the things which make students unwell. A child who is so stressed by the pressure of exams and academic achievement in their school, who worries about the state of the world, who is friendless and bullied online to the point where they develop an eating disorder or start to have suicidal thoughts, will probably not be cured by weekly mindfulness sessions led by someone well-meaning who once did a course at the local well-being/leisure/community centre. Or a self-appointed "coach" who charges by the hour.

In this scenario there is little the Department for Education (DfE) can do about the online bullies or the global warming disasters or terrorism, but they could make an enormous change around the stresses of the "relentless" drive for academic achievement and the great god *grades*. Can you really describe as a success a student who achieves straight A*s at GCSE and A Level and then is so burnt out by education that they decide they've had enough of it, or those who go on to a top university where they take their own lives? Change the stressors in schools — don't appoint people to apply emotional sticking plasters over them. That is, as the old saying goes, just rearranging the deckchairs on the *Titanic*.

But what can we as humble classroom teachers do in this scenario? It's not up to us to change the way education is structured. If we, and by extrapolation the schools in which we teach, are measured according to the existing Ofsted teaching standards, we are not in a position to step outside those standards and say, "We're not playing according to your rules." If we do, then we probably won't last very long in teaching. And that's no good for the students. So what we have to do is to look at every element of our own practice and try to alleviate the strains of modern education on the students in our care. We have to have the courage to change the things we can change.

And this is the whole point of Strictly Positive Teaching. We are working within the constraints of the system, which compels us to teach in a certain way, to help to raise the well-being of our students and, just as importantly, of ourselves.

For this reason I have organised this book according to the DfE teaching standards to show how we can employ the rules of Strictly Positive Teaching in all areas of our practice to do what we can to improve the well-being of the students in our care. Much of what you read you will think is completely obvious, and I make no apology for that. No teacher comes into the profession to wreak havoc on a student's well-being, after all. Most of what I'm advising is a tweak: looking at things from a positive perspective rather than a negative perspective, looking for and focussing on positives rather than negatives, not only in students but in ourselves as professionals, in order to do our bit to make the institutions in which we work that little bit healthier and happier.

I hope it goes without saying that the recommendations included in this book do not represent a "how to teach" prescription. Looking through this handbook should be like pausing at the Pick 'n' Mix at your local multiplex: pick what you fancy, in whatever combination you fancy, try different things, and see what suits you.

❖ Being vigilant for positives

Again, the advice to "catch them getting it right" is hardly a novel idea. But I would argue that, like the smiley face and the sad face, it is not often put into practice with enough consistency and therefore with enough impact.

There is a temptation in the teaching profession to look for errors and omissions, to be alert for negatives. This is hardly surprising since in the core business of teaching students Maths, English, French or History, what we're doing is teaching students correct facts and techniques. If a student adds 2+2 and makes 5, we need to draw their attention to the incorrect conclusion; an incorrect spelling of "begining" will become an ingrained habitual error unless at some point a teacher draws a student's attention to the missing "n"; a student will almost certainly keep failing to add feminine endings to adjectives unless a teacher tells them t o, and so forth. A failure to pick out errors and omissions is a failure to teach properly.

It stands to reason then that the same teacher would scan a class looking for behaviours that would negatively impact on the teaching and learning taking place in their lesson, as well as for errors and omissions, which they would then draw attention to.

The reverse is true of Strictly Positive Teaching. A Strictly Positive Teacher is eternally vigilant, looking for and commenting upon good behaviour and work while dealing firmly but silently with poor behaviour or work.

❖ Being the adult in a room full of children

In the same way, because we adults are charged with preparing the children in our care for adulthood, there is a temptation for schools to require students to behave as if they were adults already, rather than working with their adolescent rhythms to give them the best possible chances of success in getting there.

In the Strictly Positive Teaching model, schools would give students the best possible chances by working as far as possible with their natural inclinations, abilities and hindering factors, rather than forcing them too young to conform to adult expectations of adult behaviour.

Obviously, young people are not a homogeneous group – their natural inclinations will vary according to their age, gender, background, learning history, learning ability or disability, physical or mental ability or disability among many, *many* other factors.

However, a cursory acquaintance with child development means that we can apply certain key principles. School-age children, and yes, I mean all of them, are not mini-adults, and they are at different stages of development at different times. We would never give a seven-year-old a lesson on quadratic equations, nor would we hand picture dictionaries to our sixth formers thinking they will help them, and it's well-known that adults have a maximum attention span of 45 minutes, which is why we get fed so much coffee when we go on conferences. Yet we expect four-year-olds to sit quietly in circle time and run activities in year 10 where students sit immobile and concentrate for up to an hour.

It doesn't make sense to start from the aims of the adults in the community and then try to force the younger students into conforming with those aims, if they work contrary to children's developmental stages. Starting from this point means we are forever correcting behaviour, imposing sanctions and getting frustrated because the young people in our charge are not doing what we want them to.

In my first year of teaching I was trying to explain some nuanced point of German grammar to a year of utterly uninterested year 9s, and some of them were off-task and chatting.

Frustrated, I asked nobody in particular: "Why can't you all just be quiet and listen?"

From the first row Cheryl piped up, "Because we're children, Miss."

It doesn't sound like a eureka moment, but it was. I still remember Cheryl for this one utterance, which she had probably forgotten by break time. From then on I started trying to construct my lessons with this basic truth in mind. Obviously, there will always be times when I have to make a huge effort to bring the kids with me, and sometimes I won't be successful but I will try and keep certain fundamentals of human behaviour in mind when planning.

❖ Attention span

Take attention span, for example. Most teachers and psychologists would agree that the ability to focus and sustain attention is crucial to student success. I remember being told years ago that the maximum attention span of an adult was 45 minutes and that was long before the arrival of mobile technology and social media made instant gratification realistically possible and rendered us all more impatient. In my business career presentations would never run for more than 45 minutes at a stretch. Writing and editing this book, I have to take a break every 45 minutes.

Nowadays, according to which research you read, that average attention span has shortened to anything from 14 minutes to 8 seconds. Research conducted in 2017 for the Skipton Building Society suggested that when watching television the average British adult will focus fully only for 10 minutes before shifting focus, usually to look at a mobile phone. Motorists, scarily, will focus fully on the road for 10 minutes and then will go into autopilot. In a meeting, staff will concentrate for an average of 13 minutes before zoning out and thinking about something else. Compared with that, some estimates of a student's ability to focus in school for 10-20 minutes seem rather optimistic.

In *Engaging 'Teens and Tweens: A Brain-Compatible Approach to Reaching Middle and High School Students,* Raleigh Philp recommends 20 minutes as the maximum time a teacher can reasonably expect students to stay in a "positive learning state" without a change of stimulus.

Yet in many schools each lesson lasts an hour and if students can't manage to concentrate for all of that time then we say they're poorly behaved, rather than recognising that they're conforming to a well-known reality. Unless we want everything to fall apart in our lessons, we would be sensible to plan them to provide variety. Activities of 10-15 minutes seem a good place to go, with plenty of variety. Any more than 15 minutes and we're risking off-task behaviour.

Teenagers are biologically programmed to rebel against adult authority; they're biologically required to take risks, to be irresponsible, not to think too much about the consequences of their behaviour. Otherwise, those young Neanderthals would still be squatting in caves, clinging to Mummy Neanderthal instead of going out to dice with wild animals and risk death in order to hunt for the family, and the upshot would be that everyone would starve. Everybody accepts that teenage is a time of rebellion and pushing boundaries, but we still conflate this biological reality with kids being "difficult", by which of course we mean difficult *for us*.

Now, I'm not saying we should just expect them to be rebellious and challenging and go with it as they abuse their teachers and throw chairs all over the place but, as the adults in the room, we do need to think carefully about developmental milestones when we plan the activities we use to achieve an outcome, and consider the way in which we talk to students and the behaviour-management strategies we are going to use in our practice.

Despite my inability to explore all the aspects of Strictly Positive Teaching fully with our SLTs, I did get the chance to talk to the whole staff about positive behaviour-management techniques and I have gone into classrooms and watched these techniques being put into practice with varying degrees of success, in some cases transforming a teacher's daily practice.

They are known in vague terms to nearly everybody but not necessarily put into practice in as consistent a way as is needed for success. As with any set of techniques it's easy to try them out half-heartedly for a while and then abandon them proclaiming "they don't work" or it's "too much like hard work". Some people just plain get them wrong. But for some they have, as they did for me, transformed their classroom practice. Included in this book you will find case studies that may reflect situations you recognise, and may offer suggestions as to how you might confront similar challenges in the future.

Strictly Positive Teaching is not only about behaviour management though. I want to discuss how remaining Strictly Positive can help in every aspect of a teacher's professional practice and how, after consistency over a period of time, it can become self-sustaining, rewarding and enjoyable.

The Seven Rules of Strictly Positive Teaching:

1. *Teachers have positive expectations of learners*
2. *Teachers positively take charge*
3. *Teachers have consistent, fair methods*
4. *Positive effort, behaviour and progress are noticed and rewarded*
5. *Praise is public, specific and leads to reward; negative interaction is private, specific and leads to sanction*
6. *Positives and negatives do not cancel each other out*
7. *Teachers work with students' natures, not against them*

❖ Why attention-seeking behaviour is a teacher's friend

Children want attention. In fact, children need attention just as grass needs rain. If they cannot get positive attention, negative attention will do. In the Strictly Positive Teacher's classroom there are endless opportunities to gain positive attention, and no opportunities at all for negative attention.

Let's go back a few steps. When a child is born, it requires the attention of a prime carer for all of its needs. Wherever and whenever those needs are not met, the child will employ what strategies are at his or her disposal to attract the attention of the caregiver to have their needs met. A baby has limited options: what it does is to cry. The longer its needs remain unsatisfied, the longer it cries. Most new parents quickly develop a checklist for when their baby cries. Hungry? Feed. Tired? Put down for a nap. Windy? Burp. Wet? Change the nappy. In this way they can quickly meet the baby's needs and stop the crying. In other words: there is a need, which provokes an alert, which provokes an action to meet that need. It's a simple mechanism which works most of the time. And where the crying persists beyond these simple initial interventions, parents will usually seek help from a GP or healthcare professional to check that there is no medical reason for it.

There are some parents who, for various reasons, are unable to interact with their baby on even this basic level and then the child will develop increasingly intractable problems. But for the vast majority of parents and children, this behaviour and response is a healthy and manageable communication.

As the child develops and their needs (or perceived needs) become more complex so do the behaviours they exhibit, and so it becomes more difficult for the parents to interpret these, and problems may start to emerge. These may be to do with the quality, quantity or lack of communication; they may be to do with the quality as well as the quantity of attention – most probably they are caused by a combination of the two. Some young people in our classes appear with a history of too little attention, some with too much.

For most children, parents will more or less have got the balance of demand and response broadly right, and children will understand the way in which adults and young people interact, and will also understand that the grown-up is in charge, that that adult is benevolent and looking out for the child, and so the boundaries imposed are accepted. But not all children are in this situation, and not all children understand that the boundaries are for their own benefit.

Some children have been forced to learn through bitter experience that parents, or even all adults, are unpredictable and inconsistent. They've discovered that any behaviour can elicit all sorts of different responses, sometimes benevolent, but sometimes hostile, even dangerous; they have also often learned that they need to persist to gain an adult's attention. Some have come to believe that adult response is inconsistent and unpredictable and this inconsistency and unpredictability can be dangerous or even violent. They come to us vigilant and wary, anticipating negative responses, or needing to engage attention at all costs.

Students who manifest such difficulties to a higher degree may have an attachment disorder. These are dealt with in more detail in the context of Strictly Positive Differentiation (Chapter 8). But it is worth remembering, *always*, how attention from a teacher, and from peers, can affect any student's behaviour.

A great deal of poor behaviour is attention-seeking. Some students will want lots of attention. They need it and that need will dictate all their behaviour in your classroom. If the student can get attention for doing the right thing, then that will probably satisfy their need. That's why the boy who is terrible at everything except Maths has a bad reputation with everyone except the Maths teacher; the positive attention he gets in Maths satisfies his need. If, however, a student can't get positive attention from the teacher; if she can't keep up with what's being taught, or she's missed too much to be able to hope to understand it, or if it plain doesn't interest her, then she can get attention in one of two ways. First, she can act up until the teacher ignores the rest of the class and focusses on her. That way no one else is learning, she hears her name over and over again and she gets attention. Second, she can ignore the teacher and what they are doing in the classroom and concentrate on getting the attention of her peers. She'll start with her friends and once they're fully focussed on her she might start to attract the attention of the kids who are trying to work, or the teacher will be distracted from active teaching by trying to bring her and her friends back into line. Or there'll be an explosion when the teacher is goaded into shouting. Either way – shed-loads of attention: job done.

Attention is the objective. Positive attention is the best, but if it's not available then negative attention will do.

So a wise teacher, a Strictly Positive Teacher, will have a consistent set of positive behaviour-management strategies, which they will employ fairly in every lesson.

❖ The Teaching Standards

As things currently stand, at any stage of a teacher's career they have to be aware of the formal requirements of the DfE Teaching Standards, whether they're working to achieve Qualified Teacher Status as they embark on their teaching journey, or are near the top of the structure applying for the Upper Pay Scale. Those formal requirements are therefore a useful way of organising any array of strategies and techniques, so I have organised those of the Strictly Positive Teacher according to these eight starting points.

It is said, and I agree, that you cannot teach your lesson until you've got your behaviour management right, and so I have put Behaviour Management as one of the first areas to explore as a Strictly Positive Teacher. However, I would go back a step. I don't believe you can get your behaviour management right until you have formed healthy and positive classroom relationships with the students in your care. I have therefore added my own teaching standard – Relationship Building – at the moment included in TS7, the standard that deals with Behaviour Management. I think that while all schools recognise that these relationships are crucial to the smooth running of classrooms and schools, not enough is made of the skills and techniques that can be learned, practised and honed like any other skill. Relationships underpin absolutely everything – as a teacher, the quality of the professional classroom relationships you form with students will dictate your teaching success or lack of it.

So this book is organised with the Teaching Standards in mind, but in the order in which I believe the standards need to be mastered:

- *Relationships (TS7)*
- *Behaviour Management (TS7)*
- *Expectations (TS1)*
- *Progress and Outcomes (TS2)*
- *Pedagogy, Curriculum and Subject Knowledge (TS3)*
- *Lesson Planning and Teaching (TS4)*
- *Differentiation (TS5)*
- *Assessment (TS6)*
- *Professional Collaboration and Cooperation (TS8)*

1

WHAT IS STRICTLY POSITIVE TEACHING?

Wait... **Strict AND Positive?**

Okay, I know what you're thinking: "Strictly Positive Teaching" – there are three words that don't belong together. First, you can either be strict or positive; you are either a strict teacher, or you are a positive Pollyanna.

Strict teachers come in different forms. There are obviously amalgams, but here are three types you might recognise.

The Tyrannical Teacher

Given the choice, most teachers would probably opt for being the tyrannical teacher. Tyrants can get a lot done, and check a lot of boxes, because there is no messing with them. If you are a strict teacher, you rule your classroom with a rod of iron, you are vigilant for any whisper out of turn or misbehaviour of any sort, and you have silence in the room until you deem there should be sound. On your terms. Lord help the child who was shattered after a late away game and didn't get your homework done – you brook no excuses. Rules are rules, after all.

You are probably the one who can't imagine why other colleagues empathise with each other about the impossibility of dealing with Katie in year 9.

"She's fine for me," you think, but wisely don't say because you know it will get your colleagues' collective back up. "All you have to do is apply the behaviour policy," you go on to say to yourself. "How hard can it be?"

You find it hard to understand why everyone doesn't do it the way you do. Students know not to come to you with excuses or reasons for omissions or infractions – they know this isn't a democracy and you don't go in for pointless conversations. Your name is against many students in the detention hall each day. You are widely known as a disciplinarian, and that is a good thing. You are usually popular with older students, whereas younger children regard you with abject terror.

Okay, sometimes kids feel a sanction is unfair; sometimes they might not like you much, but hey, what self-respecting teacher needs the approval of a 15-year-old? You didn't come into this profession to win any popularity contests. When the kids leave with brilliant results they'll thank you. And they probably will. You are an excellent teacher. But you're not kind, and sometimes you are unfair. They will never forget or forgive the perceived injustices, but whatever the discussions they have about you when they meet for a reunion in a dark pub at an age when their school-days are the stuff of nostalgia, they will finish with "...but s/he was a bloody good teacher."

The Miserable Teacher

You're probably not the strict teacher that young people actively dislike. You shouldn't really be in teaching at all, because you don't really like children at all, but you've been put on this earth to ensure that recalcitrant kids get through the course and come out the other end with a decent grade. You've been teaching for years and, frankly, you don't need any keen young beginner coming in and introducing new ways of doing things when you've been getting kids good grades since 1993.

Since you don't particularly want to do anything fancy in your lessons, you maintain order with rigorous discipline based upon pre-emptive application of the behaviour policy. None of this "three strikes and you're out" nonsense. If pupils muck about, they'll be punished. If they're on the fringes of the mucking about, they'll get the same sanction; you don't go in for too much discussion and you haven't got time to go deciding who is the real culprit in a situation. No one much likes you because you're a grumpy bugger, and you are regarded as extremely unfair. And no one really thinks much of you as a teacher. You think you're funny, but sarcasm doesn't go across very well with kids.

The Shouter

Then there are the strict teachers who are shouters. Blessed with generous volume controls and the power to project formidably, if they were animated in cartoon form they would be the ones whose voice could blow their students' hair horizontal. They tend to punish less than they shout because filling in forms and placing kids in detention is a lot slower and more laborious than just having a good shout, but the actual shouting itself is so unpleasant and even distressing to students that the possibility of it occurring serves as a deterrent in itself. Shouters tend to be a little moody and unpredictable, and they think of themselves as "characters", as do most of the students. They tend to be energetic teachers who work hard for their students, and they are always tired and always living life on a knife-edge. When they shout, it is not always the stage-managed acting that many teachers go in for, but sometimes a real eruption of anger and frustration, in the course of which they may make unguarded, potentially career-limiting statements.

On the other side of the fence, you have:

Positive Pollyanna

If you're Positive Pollyanna, as far as you're concerned you and the kids are all in this together. You shower unfocussed praise around: "That's fantastic! Well done, you!" – and pretend not to notice the tussling between Tom and Sayed in the corner of the room as they flick each other increasingly vigorously with the double-sided, beautifully illustrated, carefully constructed worksheet that you were up until 11.27pm last night preparing. You're hurt that they don't appreciate your efforts, and sometimes you might be moved to say so. Sometimes you praise kids who are actively misbehaving or avoiding doing any work, in the misplaced belief that this niceness will shame them into complying with your wishes.

Sometimes another teacher will storm into your classroom shouting for order and then recover their composure when they see you perched next to a student, facilitating. They hadn't realised a teacher was in the room – it was that noisy.

But kids love you. You're often told that, and it gives you a lovely warm fuzzy feeling. You're so nurturing and friendly, unfailingly smiling and doing absolutely everything in your power to ensure your classroom is a place of joy and creativity. When kids act up you are personally wounded, a fact which you share with the miscreants, who are paralysed with embarrassment when they think you might actually cry in their presence. (Because you have in the past done exactly that, and word gets around.) They will be subjected to hard stares from other students who come to your aid and comfort you. They will feel awful. Because they really don't want to upset you. But next time they come in they'll forget and start mucking around again in unstructured moments. Not because they don't like you – they really do. But they're kids. They'd just like things to be a bit more focussed. In that pub you will be remembered with great affection, and a tiny bit of mockery.

In truth, the vast majority of us are probably somewhere in between the above stereotypes, and we have our own strategies and methods of teaching and managing behaviour in our classes. We get on well with our students generally. Some days we'll ace all our lessons and our behaviour management will be spot-on. Occasionally we'll have a dreadful lesson, or even a dreadful day, and we'll moan, possibly shout a bit, then get over ourselves, calm down and plan a better day tomorrow.

The Strictly Positive Teacher

By contrast, the Strictly Positive teaching model is a very simple one. It enables teachers to be both strict and positive at the same time. This is effected by a very simple tweak in teacher thinking. In short, by all that s/he says or does, the Strictly Positive Teacher shows that what matters is what the students are doing *right*, and not what they are doing wrong. Praise is *specific*. Whereas no good contribution, enhanced effort or courteous gesture goes unnoticed or unheralded, sanctions are applied rigorously, consistently, but without a word in lesson time.

The Strictly Positive Teacher is vigilant, aware of everything that is going on in the class, alert to everything that is going right in the class, and quietly to what is going wrong, too. They address what is going right and what is going wrong swiftly and deftly. So far, so same as before. The change is that what is going right is dealt with loudly and publicly in full view of the class, and what is going wrong is acknowledged silently, deferred, and dealt with privately.

If you go into the classroom of a successful Strictly Positive Teacher, the names you hear will be the names of those who are behaving, achieving, being courteous and doing well. Students are confident that effort, contribution and risk-taking will be recognised and celebrated. They are confident that what they can do is much more important to the teacher than what they can't do. They know that what they're doing right is more important to the teacher than what they, or others, are doing wrong. They know it is better to try and fail, than not to try. They also know that any disruption of their learning will be dealt with swiftly.

2

STRICTLY POSITIVE RELATIONSHIP BUILDING

The Strictly Positive Teacher has in mind the mental health and well-being of their students, and wants to ensure they are acting in a way that works with students' natures. They know that in order to maintain a good positive atmosphere within the classroom, and thereby be in a position to be able to teach the lesson, they must first establish positive relationships *with* their students, and foster positive relationships *between* students. This is surely at the heart of positive teaching – mental health depends on relationships; good relationships foster good mental health, while poor relationships are unsettling and destructive. For our most vulnerable students, poor relationships may be the norm in their everyday home lives, and could perhaps be all they know. In the face of such a background, the positive relationship with their teachers may effect a considerable and visible difference in their behaviour, learning and mental health.

A 2016 report from the University of Cambridge found that students who had a positive relationship with their teacher displayed 18% more "prosocial" behaviour towards their peers, and up to 10% even two years later. They also manifested up to 38% less aggressive behaviour (and 9% up to four years later). Positivity towards their teacher was also seen in 56% less "oppositional defiant" behaviour, such as argumentativeness and vindictiveness towards authority figures. The effect of a positive attitude towards their teacher on infant school pupils had already been demonstrated in earlier studies. It makes sense then that a Strictly Positive Teacher would do well to think carefully about every aspect of their classroom relationships.

Positive relationships start from a clear understanding of how the classroom works, of everybody's place within the room and their rights and responsibilities. Relationships, any relationships, are built on trust and it is essential that everyone in that room trusts that the conditions will be created by the adult in the room – the teacher – for everybody to feel safe enough to learn effectively.

Building positive relationships with students emphatically does not mean acting as if they are your friends, or trying to cultivate egalitarian rapports. You are the authority figure, and they will look to you to sort out anything that goes wrong with the relationships within the room. Positive relationships are ones where everyone treats one another with courtesy and consideration. A light touch and humour are always appreciated by students, but not at the expense of order and respect.

Fostering positive relationships between students takes more effort. There may be more than 30 of them and there's one of you, maybe two if you have a Learning Support Assistant (LSA) or a Teaching Assistant (TA) in the room. Pastoral leaders and behaviour managers are always hearing about fallings-out or bullying that is conducted within a lesson. Sometimes the first moment at which a teacher becomes aware of conflict is at the moment when actual physical violence erupts. Conflict between students in our classrooms happens to all of us at some time or other, but if it happens frequently in your lessons, then your teacher antenna needs a bit of rejigging. No one is suggesting that all lessons need to be teacher-led from the front in order to avoid the possibility of conflict arising between students, but when you set a group or pairs exercise, or embark on a task that involves movement, it is important that you gauge the temperature of the relationships in the room. If you spot a storm gathering, you need to intervene; in some cases, it may be necessary to change your lesson plan to head off conflict.

Experienced teachers develop a radar that can warn of advancing problems – until they have reached this point, colleagues need to learn to look around often and "read the room", which is difficult when you're beside a child explaining the niceties of the agricultural revolution. Think Meerkat – bob up every now and then and have a good scan of the class.

❖ Maintain good relationships with pupils

I had a teacher when I was at school who believed that all she needed to do to make someone do something was maintain piercing eye contact, move slightly closer than was completely comfortable and then issue the instruction slowly, distinctly and very, very emphatically. This strategy was absolutely intended to be menacing and to emphasise the power imbalance between us. It made me want to disobey her, and I was a relatively cooperative student. So I deliberately didn't try as hard in her lessons as I would for the other teachers with whom I had a more positive relationship.

Fast forward a couple of decades and in business I met a manager who was brought up in the same school of behaviour management. He employed the same tactics dressed up with a couple of extra words, and I felt equally disinclined to do what he said, even if he did follow it up, as per the manual, with a "thank you" before he moved away. I didn't like either of them, and I did not want to do anything that they wanted me to do. Obviously I *should have* done what each of them told me to do, but I deliberately didn't do it as well as I could have done. The only person who suffered was me, but I probably didn't achieve my potential in Chemistry, which probably didn't reflect well on my teacher.

On EduTwitter I read a lot of discussion about how teachers shouldn't need to be liked by students; they should simply be able to expect obedience and compliance in their classes, and schools should have ways of dealing with the students if they don't comply as expected. And I agree. There must be an expectation that compliance and obedience is the norm in a class, and there must be backup for any classroom teacher that kicks in when the absence of these two things means that the learning is threatened.

However, just because you think things *should* be a certain way, that doesn't mean they will be. I tend to prefer a pragmatic view of things which says that if a teacher can do something positive to manage their classroom and be seen as much as possible as a positive, fair, benign authority within that classroom, not a step on the way to the real authority, the manager who takes over the issue when the student has left the room, then that will pay dividends. Apart from anything, every time a student leaves your room they miss teaching points, and when they come in the next time they're behind the others, which increases the likelihood that they'll act up in order to mask the fact of their being behind, so sending a child out can negatively affect behaviour in the next lesson with that child. Equally, no teacher wants to be seen as a soft touch – in order to *have* authority in your classroom you have to *exert* authority in your classroom. Deal with things as the authority and you *are* the authority. Exercising authority here doesn't mean scattering around sanctions like confetti, but taking charge of what happens in the room and having positive strategies to do so.

Thompson (1998) says: "The most powerful weapon available to secondary teachers who want to foster a favorable learning climate is a positive relationship with our students."

If you have to share a classroom with 30 young people, it's an awful lot easier to get things done if there is an understanding between you, a tacit contract that you will treat one another with respect, that the students will let the teacher teach, and the teacher will help the students learn. To a large degree you as a teacher are the one who creates that contract and is responsible for its terms. Yes, a school will have policies governing every area of school life, but within the classroom it's you and the kids, and it's a wise teacher who takes that on board and works with it. Just because kids *should* behave without necessarily liking or respecting their teacher, that doesn't necessarily mean they *will*. The energy expended in creating positive relationships will result in a reduced likelihood that you'll have to invoke the higher levels of the school behaviour policy and will probably mean less disruption to your class.

Marzano (2003) reports that students will resist rules and procedures along with the consequent disciplinary actions if the foundation of a good relationship is lacking.

More positively, John Hattie (Visible Learning for Teachers, 2015) discovered that teachers are likely to have a much greater impact on the learning of their students if they forge strong relationships with them.

So what are the Strictly Positive Starting Steps to forging positive classroom relationships?

1. *Forget all that nonsense about not smiling until half-term. Smile. You chose this profession, presumably because at least to some degree you enjoy the company of young people. Let it show. If you don't like young people, don't go into teaching. Do research or something.*

2. *See the students as people, with all the troubles and joys, strengths and weaknesses, good days and bad days as anyone*

else. As you yourself, for instance. If you have a shouty day, or a moany day, or a can't-be-bothered day, it's unlikely you would expect people to draw the conclusion that you are a shouty/moany/can't-be-bothered sort of person. You will instead attribute it to the fact that you had a row with your partner, or you pranged your car, or you received sad news about your friend who lives in Peru, or your guinea pig died. If you behave in a similar way on several concurrent days, you would put it down to a run of bad luck, probably not to a character flaw or failing, something that needs to be disciplined out of you. Extend the same logic to students. You don't know what's happening in their lives.

3. Greet them at the door. As students come into your domain you have a chance to make eye contact with them, smile, let them know they're coming into your environment and that everything will be fine. Especially if the last lesson you shared did not go well, your smile and that eye contact tells them that this is a new start, and with a clean slate.

4. Create a structured environment with clear, sensible, consistently and fairly applied rules and routines. Students like to know where they are with a teacher. Nothing will turn a student into a rebel like unfairness. Except chaos – chaos would make Peter Perfect riot... If students understand the reasons for rewards and sanctions, and they trust the teacher to apply them sensibly, they will accept them. A structured environment where the teacher is trusted to do the right thing by the students makes them feel safe. Chaos is no fun for anyone.

5. Be positive. Any of the Strictly Positive techniques or strategies in this book will lead you to show yourself as a positive person and this will go a long way towards good classroom relationships.

6. Teach with passion and enthusiasm. Hopefully you love your subject. Hopefully you love teaching. Hopefully you really want the students to love your subject and you want to communicate that through making your lessons fun or interesting (and interesting is fun, after all; fun isn't just gimmicks).

7. Be interested in students as human beings with a life outside your class. If a student has been named in assembly, or you've heard

about some success in a football match, or winning an award for charitable work or playing in a concert, congratulate them on it. If they mention something in the course of your lesson, show an interest in their work with St John's Ambulance, or busking outside the cinema, or cycling to a nearby town. Ask a question; it is unlikely the student will want to embark on a long conversation, but in the three seconds the interchange took as they passed you on the way into class or as you work your way around the room, you'll have increased their trust in you. Don't quiz them as if you're the Spanish Inquisition, and don't try to be too interested; that's just creepy. Use a light touch.

8. *In class, involve everyone so that everyone feels equally welcome. Try not to go down the route of calling only upon those with their hands up who look as if they'll burst if you don't invite them to respond. Make everyone feel present in the lesson and valued.*

9. *Have high expectations of all. If you reserve your challenge for those who constantly put their hands up, who are on paper the high performers, the visible people in the room, the others will recognise that you have low expectations of them and will switch off. High expectations does not mean the same expectations; if you know your students you can pitch expectations individually – high for them.*

10. *At the end of the class make a point of praising anyone who did particularly well this lesson, and have a quiet word with those who did poorly, ensuring there is a plan for the next lesson, and that they leave you with a good memory. They need to know that, for better or for worse, you recognise them.*

Developing positive relationships with your students is the most important first step to establishing positive behaviour management, and creating a positive environment for learning. Arguably, it is a prerequisite for learning.

Most employees are more likely to want to try to impress a boss that they like, rather than one they think treats them unfairly and doesn't treat them with respect. In the same way, students will like and respect a teacher who shows like and respect towards them. The key result of this like and respect is that they are much more likely to do what you want them to do, because they want to please you. So it is your positive relationship which causes them to behave appropriately within the boundaries of the rules in your classroom: they are not obeying the rules; they are obeying *you*.

Alfie Kohn, in *Beyond Discipline,*1996, says: "Children are more likely to be respectful when important adults in their lives respect them. They are more likely to care about others if they know they are cared about."

Let's look at some of the prerequisites of good relationships in a little more detail.

❖ Positive expectations

Educational rule #1: students live up or down to their teachers' expectations of them.

Educational rule #2: students live up or down to their teachers' expectations of them.

Educational rule #3: students live up or down to their teachers' expectations of them.

Yes, it's that important. Study upon study, over many decades, shows that expectations of low or high achievement by their students become self-fulfilling. Teachers who communicate explicit or implicit high expectations to their students will find those expectations met. Conversely, those who implicitly communicate low expectations will turn students off, making them rebellious and negative. Some will counter this with some stern warnings about expectations being set too high, and of course that can be a temptation, but we're professionals – we know what high enough is for an individual.

As the popular meme has it: "If you think you can, or you think you can't, you're probably right."

Try not to listen to other teachers when they dismiss a student. While it is tempting to go into your first meeting with Ryan in 9F with a plan of attack, anticipating the worst, it won't be a good start for either of you. Ryan probably expects to be hauled up quickly by every teacher he encounters. It's practically his stock in trade. Try to treat him like every other student; he may surprise you. Look out for something positive in him. Comment on it briefly and move on. Don't allow him to think you're getting him onside just because you've heard of his reputation (even though you may be), but just be as positive with him as you are with the others.

The Strictly Positive teaching model, which leads teachers to explicit recognition of positive expectations, whether in behaviour or academic terms, by *all* students, will lead students to share those high expectations and recognise their own steps towards them. Obviously this does not mean you have the *same* expectations of each student, but you should aim to allow each student to push at the boundaries of their own abilities.

I know that an argument rages within UK education as to whether Learning Objectives (LO) are worth the whiteboard space they're written on. I read recently that it was a scandal that three minutes out of a lesson should be used to write objectives in books. But I'm going to speak out in favour of the lowly LO. If you agree with me that the crucial thing about any lesson is that students should have acquired knowledge, understanding or skills *which they did not have when they walked into the room*, then learning objectives, which build through a unit of work and which students can see progression within and between units, will enable them to make sense of their learning and render it relevant.

You'll probably be bored reading this by the end of this book, even if you just dip into it from time to time, because I'm going to repeat it like a mantra. At the end of every single lesson they ever do, a student should leave the classroom being able to do something they couldn't do or knowing something they didn't know when they walked in.

Within each lesson, where a generic learning objective framed as an "I can..." statement may be what is recorded in books, teachers can have quick words with specific students or groups of students as to the specifics of what they want them to be able to do.

So, for instance, if the learning objective in a French lesson were "I can use the imperfect and perfect tenses in a description of a past holiday," you might drop by the desks of a group of four talented students and say, "I'd like you to refer to yourself and other people in your description." And to a couple who are struggling, say: "I'd like you to write two sentences in the perfect tense saying what activities you did, and two sentences starting with 'c'etait', describing how you felt about the activities."

By having this quick word with them, each student should feel you're taking enough notice to ask them to do their best.

Another issue around expectations is that of data versus the evidence of your own eyes. We are all professionals and should be combining the two. We do all we can to use everything at our disposal to prepare suitable lessons for all in our classes and to moderate our expectations upwards or downwards. If those data expectations look wrong, consider why. Is there something going wrong in that student's life? Was there something wrong when the student did the tests that yielded this data? Consult pastoral staff.

❖ Everybody participates

All students need to be treated equitably. This emphatically does not mean that all students should be treated the same. But all students should feel they are fairly treated in the classroom, and part of that is that they should all feel the teacher is including them in the lesson.

There are some students who can go a whole day without being asked a single question in any lesson. They do this by employing twin strategies: a) they don't put their hands up, and b) they don't draw attention to themselves by any misbehaviour. Some of these children, knowing they won't be called upon, decide there is no necessity for them to concentrate on what's going on, and they can dismantle their pen, think about their new computer game or ponder their lunch choices instead. Unsurprisingly, they may then make "less than expected progress".

In your classroom it would be wise for students to assume they will need to answer a question at some point in your class. If they don't expect to be asked a question, if they have grown accustomed to not being called upon, while a small cohort of keen and enthusiastic students handle all the questions, they may not bother to pay attention in the lessons that follow. When you don't ask questions of some students in your class, you communicate that you don't expect them to be able to answer your questions. This may or may not be your intention, but they'll assume you expect *more* of those few who do answer all the questions, whose hands are always up and who are always called upon to answer. They will then come to believe that those other students are more able than they are, and they will gradually lose interest. And this in turn could trick you, as the teacher, into believing this as well.

Students develop confidence if they sense that you trust them to get the answer right, and this is compounded when they do get the answer right. In addition, making sure everyone participates in every single lesson means behaviour improves, as students understand that they need to be on task and ready to answer at all times.

There are several ways of ensuring everyone participates:

1. *Everyone answers the same question: this is a useful strategy for questions inviting open-ended answers, so that students can give an answer that accurately reflects their level of understanding. Making it clear that the selection of answerer will be random – rattling your trusty tub of named lolly sticks; putting up the random name generator wheel on the projector screen; or simply scanning the room wondering out loud who hasn't been given the chance to contribute much yet – clearly ask the question. Tell them no one will answer yet, and that you will give a specific length of "thinking time" – 10 seconds, 30 seconds, a minute – during which time everyone needs to come up with an answer. This is silent time for everyone. As you silently time the allotted moments, prompt anyone who looks as if they may be struggling, and assist. At the end of the time, reinforce that you now need everyone to have an answer. Start off by asking a student, someone somewhere between the most keen and the least, to answer the question to set the scene, or go absolutely random if you think it appropriate, and then go from there.*

2. *Simple to complex: once you have asked a question, give a short thinking time. Then start off by asking the simplest version of the question to reluctant students, and then continue questioning, varying the level of difficulty, up to the most confident: this way the thinking time is extended for the keener students and everyone gets to show what they can do. In other words, at the end of your lesson the students can all say, "I can..." to an appropriate level.*

3. *Modelling for assistance: this is good for repetitive questions, such as simple utterances in Modern Foreign Language (MFL). In this model you ask the more confident learners first, and the others listen and use the first confident utterances to help frame their own responses. For instance, the teacher may ask, "As-tu des frères ou des soeurs?" There will be a range of answers, most starting "J'ai un/une...". By the time the weakest student is required to answer, they will have heard some 28 variations on the theme, and should be able to formulate their own.*

4. *Encouragement to excel: where appropriate, challenge answers to questions. Perhaps smile encouragingly and use silent hand gestures to elicit expanded answers or elaboration. Perhaps ask explicitly for more. Perhaps, where an atmosphere of trust has been created, encourage other learners to seek explanation or elaboration.*

5. *Random name selection: whether you use lolly sticks in a jar or a web-based application dressed up as a wheel of fortune, or a typewriter, producing your random name generator as you set students off on a timed task is an excellent way of encouraging everyone to step up to the task they've been set. At the end of the allotted time, check everyone has finished preparing and then select randomly. You can remove the name once someone has responded, or leave them there. Either way, this genuinely random method ensures all work*

❖ Thinking time

A key element of making students positive enough to feel they can volunteer is to give "thinking time". Thinking time must be for everyone, otherwise you convey a negative message. When you pose a question in class, give thinking time. This can work in several ways.

1. *A couple of seconds: "What do you think of this (wait for a count of one...two...) Holly?" The idea is that everyone in the class, as they don't know who will be called upon, takes a moment to come up with an answer. Maybe they will down tools once Holly has answered, but you can have a rapid-fire approach: "What do you think of Holly's answer (one...two...) Josh?"*

2. *Thirty seconds to a minute: "Pens down, no talking. Thirty seconds to come up with a full sentence answer to this question: 'what is the difference between a timeframe and a tense?'" Specific expectation that everyone will have an answer to what could be a tricky question.*

3. *Until all hands are up: "Think about the question. Put your hands up when you have an answer." Wait until all or nearly all have their hands up – students will recognise that you are patient and they can't opt out of what's happening in the class.*

The important thing is that all students expect to be called upon, so all students *THINK*.

❖ Positive affirmation

Okay, I know I keep banging on about this, and I'm barely getting started, but really, it's so important it's not surprising it keeps cropping up in all sorts of areas.

If you notice when a child gets things right, when they're excelling, exceeding their own expectations and yours, challenging themselves, working harder than usual, behaving better than usual, and if you express your pleasure at all these achievements, then your relationship with that child will be better than their relationship with the teacher whose focus is always on what's going wrong and who is misbehaving. They will be grateful to you and that gratitude will manifest itself in a visible desire to maintain that good work and behaviour to carry on getting that praise and having that good relationship.

❖ Turning a negative conversation into a strictly positive one

So you've kept Joe, or Leah, or Sam back after a lesson where they pushed you to the point where you had to issue a detention. You didn't engage in discussion about it in the lesson, but now is the time.

This is the point at which you have an opportunity a) to confirm that the student understands what they did wrong, and b) to ensure that they know what to do to avoid a repetition.

Every conversation, according to Susan Scott in *Fierce Conversations*, can lead you closer to a goal or take you further away from it, so it pays to enter into it mindfully. The first advantage you have is that you have delayed the conversation about the student's error or omission until now, when they don't have the fuel of an audience. The second is that the student is now as keen as you are to keep this conversation brief. Keener.

Remember what you want from this conversation, and keep it Strictly Positive.

Ask the student to confirm that they understand the system.

"You do understand that you left me with no choice but to give you a detention, don't you?"

Either they will say yes, or bluster, in which case you will recap the system.

"You were talking when I was explaining how to use the sewing machine. So you couldn't learn from what I was saying and nor could Josh. I put your name on the board, and then you started again. I quietly directed your attention to the tick on the board but you carried on again later. So I had to put another tick on."

If more bluster...

"I've explained the rules. You know I won't say your name. It's your responsibility to be aware of what's going on."

Once you get confirmation of understanding, you can move onto your second objective.

"Now, how are we going to stop this happening again?"

There follows a brief conversation (they are keen to get away), and you will probably have some agreement about how the next lesson will proceed. This may involve a prompt as they enter the room next time, or your tapping on the desk when their name is on the board, just to give them a bit of an extra reminder. It is something between you – a sign that you want to help.

Or how about: *"Let's make a deal."*

"Let's make a deal – if you do well in the next lesson I'll put two credits on the system..."

"Let's make a deal – if you do well in the next lesson, I'll email someone about how well you've done. Who would you like me to send it to?"

"Let's make a deal. If you do well next lesson, I'll put you in charge of the bell for a week."(This is the bell I use to get silence when too many people are talking, but it could be any classroom privilege.)

If this is a repeat, or repeat-repeat occurrence, you might suggest some changes that you could make. These are changes which you, the teacher, wish to make, but it is important that the students see that there is a reason for it – it is not a punishment:

"Would it help if we changed the seating plan? Is there anywhere you could sit which would help you work better? Who could you sit next to who would help you work?"

Or:

"How about if you brought your book to me at the end of every lesson to show me how you've done in the lesson? Would that help you focus on your work? I could just give a quick comment – would that be enough to get you to focus?"

When the student leaves your room they should be thinking not about the sanction you have just applied, but the way in which you, their teacher, have put yourself out to help them succeed in your classroom. And given them choices.

❖ What if you really don't like the students in your class?

Teaching is a profession; it is a job. The relationships we have in the classroom are professional relationships, not personal ones, and as such need to be managed carefully and dispassionately. This can be difficult as the people with whom we spend our days are children and some of them can be challenging, sometimes deliberately so. It is sometimes easy to overlook the fact that these sometimes disruptive people are our clients, the people to whom we provide a service, and our job is to teach all of them to the best of our ability. It is essential that we, as the adults, act rationally and maintain our professionalism at all times.

I was worried when, not so long ago, I heard a young colleague mutter that she "hated" the class she was about to teach, that she had to struggle to maintain her temper with them, that they got under her skin. I was worried because she had uttered similar negative thoughts about other classes and this seemed like a self-fulfilling prophecy. Her lessons were becoming grim affairs, her dislike of the classes seeping out. She went into the classroom alert for poor behaviour and hostility and so, of course, she found it everywhere.

"Miss, I don't get it. I'm so confused."

"I've explained it. What is there not to get?"

"I just don't get it."

"What don't you get?"

"All of it."

"Well, I've explained it. Just get on with your work."

"But..."

"JUST GET ON WITH YOUR WORK!"

She was so convinced it was an us-and-them situation that she never considered that maybe she *wasn't* explaining things very well, that maybe it *might* be a good idea to see if she could find another way to make them understand. More importantly, she took it personally. This poorly expressed lack of understanding was, in her mind, an attempt to undermine her, to make her look foolish, to spoil the lesson she had spent so long preparing. By this attitude not only was she setting herself in opposition to the students, but by believing it was the students who were at fault and not she herself, she disempowered herself and told herself there was nothing she could do about it.

She was spending far too much time on the lesson and not nearly enough on the relationships.

If it is a truism that you cannot teach a class until you have established effective behaviour management, it is equally true that you cannot establish effective behaviour management until you have formed a healthy relationship with that class.

So how do you do that?

❖ You can decide to like a class

It is fine to lie through your teeth and tell a class you like them, and it can have amazing results. If a class who can be tricky has a single good lesson with you, how about telling them that they are in danger of becoming one of your favourite groups? Look at the faces and see if it has had an impact. In the next lesson, open the door and greet them with a big smile and a hello. Greet them warmly as individuals as you admit them. Act as if you really like them.

Go through your normal entry procedures but do it all with goodwill and warmth, engaging individuals in brief dialogue. Recap the behaviour management system but with massive emphasis on the positive side. Get going with some positives straight away.

You employ the "Act as if" strategy. In other words, you behave as if you like them in order to come to like them.

1. *Decide to like them*

2. *Tell them you like them*

3. *Smile as if you like them*

4. *Apply the behaviour management strategies consistently and dispassionately*

5. *"Act as if" is a powerful strategy for building relationships.*

We've all been there – that knot in the stomach when you have to face 8S again. The faces that swim into your head, those of the students who need somehow to be "managed", to be cajoled into compliance or manoeuvred quickly through the sanction escalation ladder until you can send them out of the room and heave a sigh of relief; the hours spent preparing lessons which you seriously doubt will go according to plan either because of those three or four "characters" whose express intent is to derail every class they're in, or the incessant off-task chat which means you have to spend the whole lesson quieting the room and re-establishing the environment necessary for successful teaching and learning to take place. The recognition that sometimes you wait for something to go wrong and therefore it does go wrong.

Most of 8S are perfectly likeable cooperative students who would like nothing more than for those irritating peers to pipe down and let them get on with the business of learning. They may feel much of the time that they attract very little attention, positive or otherwise; their teachers are so keen to manage the miscreants that it is their names which are heard in the classroom, in a positive as well as a negative context, and the silent majority barely get a look-in.

The good news is it doesn't have to be like that. A shift in focus can result in a very different view of things. You can learn to like the class.

Take a few minutes to re-evaluate the situation. Look at a list of the students in 8S and write down the names of all the students who are cooperative and appropriately behaved. If possible, use your school's information system to collate photographs of these students, and really concentrate on them. Ignore the others. Perhaps you can asterisk the students who are actively engaged in the class, whose work is good and who could do well in your subject. Then decide to teach *them*. Prepare your next lesson to focus on them. Visualise their faces as you prepare the lesson. Marvel at what a nice class 8S is – how could you not have noticed this before!

(As for the others, have a word with any necessary colleagues. As you are not going to engage with the disruptive students, it is likely that some of them may leave the room quite swiftly and you will need places for them to go. Just for this lesson.)

When the lesson starts, look out at those kids you have chosen to focus on, take a deep breath and smile at them. Even if it feels forced, still smile. It won't show. If you are the kind of teacher who is comfortable with such honesty, have a word with the class and tell them explicitly that today you will be focussing on all the good work that happens in the classroom.

"Right, year 8. I'm sorry that some of your lessons recently have been disrupted by the poor behaviour of a few. From today I am teaching you, those members of 8S who have not had enough of my attention. If anybody gets in the way of your learning, they will be removed from the room."

Recap your behaviour management system. You are looking for good behaviour – poor behaviour and poor work ethic will be dealt with silently and it may be that some students will need to be removed.

If you are uncomfortable with such directness, let your actions speak for you.

Look at the faces on which you have decided to focus your attention and start to narrate the good behaviour, attitude and work that is happening already in the classroom. Note it publicly: exclaim regularly at clever insights, feats of memory, joined up thinking, scholarly explanation, spontaneous note-taking, naming those responsible for such greatness and writing them up positively for all this good.

(Just for now, try to ignore the students who are not going to get your attention by poor behaviour – you have enough to do working with the cooperative majority.)

It may be, however, that some of the students who were not on your list start to get the idea and may behave and work positively. By all means mention them positively, but don't let your delight make you more effusive about them than the others; they must not think they can take over by brief bursts of cooperation.

At some point you will give the students a task to do which means you will not be teaching, explaining or modelling from the front, and you will have a chance to look around your room. Look at those students for whom you planned this lesson, look at the names written up on the board and the sense of engagement among the students whom you are teaching.

At the end of the lesson, look at the board and say the names of those who have done particularly well. Ask a few to stay behind for a moment. Don't say why.

When the others have gone, reiterate how well they have done, and what a great lesson they have had.

As Johann Wolfgang von Goethe said some 250 years ago: "*If you treat an individual as he is, he will remain how he is. But if you treat him as if he were what he ought to be and could be, he will become what he ought to be and could be.*"

The same goes for groups. That stonking great lie you told them about liking them at the beginning is, all of a sudden, transformed into shining truth.

❖ Exercise appropriate authority and act decisively when necessary

Before we move on to talk about how Strictly Positive Behaviour Management works, it needs to be explicitly stated that classroom behaviour management must be underpinned by a robust escalation policy and supported by middle and senior leaders.

Good middle and senior leaders will be useful in supporting the teacher who offers praise, and schools would be well advised to provide a reward ladder which places at least as much emphasis on praise as on sanction.

A classroom with some thirty students in it, in which a teacher is trying to teach material that the students need to learn within a defined time frame is *not* the place for negative conversations. A class where everyone is focussed on the learning for 90-100% of the time is going to be more successful than one where the learning is the focus for only 60-70% of the time. It is therefore obvious that although classroom teachers have good solid behaviour-management techniques in their armoury, it is essential that middle and senior leaders should step in promptly at the point where sanctions need to be escalated, and remove the student who is causing the disruption.

This serves a few purposes: it swiftly removes the interruption to the learning and keeps the class's focus on the teacher and the learning. It also signals to students who have stepped out of line that they are not in opposition to the individual teacher, but rather offending against the school and, most importantly, their peers.

Teachers will do all they can to develop and promote positive teacher-student relationships, starting from a point where they are positively the authority in the room. It is they who will decide what happens in that space – preferably to practise good, positive behaviour-management techniques. But if these efforts fail, as they sometimes do, then they will want to act decisively and escalate swiftly so as to minimise any extra disruption to the class. A warning and two strikes seems appropriate leeway to allow a student to change their behaviour. After that it is wholly appropriate that they should be moved or removed.

"I was only... and then the teacher... for no reason at all. I didn't do anything..."

We've all heard variations on this theme. How many times has a tutor or pastoral leader, in conversation after the event with a student about an incident that has occurred in a classroom, heard that student attempt to shift blame to the teacher? The teacher is always picking on them; the teacher is unable to control the class; the teacher has misread a situation and overreacted unfairly. It is that leader's responsibility to guide the student to recognise their responsibility in these situations. If they see the student often after incidents in several classrooms with several teachers, it should be easier to make that student realise the common factor is their own behaviour and attitude. (Although I have met students who told me this is only evidence that *all* their teachers get together to concoct a common story in order to get them chucked out. Not many have asserted this but a couple have!)

Students who are frequently in trouble with authority in schools tend to be those who fail to connect their own behaviour with the sanctions imposed. This is where a universally applied standard of behaviour management can help, one that is explicit and visible. We won't be able to help all students, and there will still be some who will decide that "this school" is the problem. They may not even accept responsibility when they go to another school and discover things are just as "unfair" there. They simply cannot arrive at the obvious conclusion: that it is they themselves who are at fault, and the solution to the situation in which they find themselves therefore lies within them.

Whatever techniques are employed within a teacher's classroom, if an individual pupil proves resistant to any or all of them, there should *always* be other people whom that teacher can call upon and expect to attend promptly when needed. Students should be fully aware of what a school's behaviour system entails, and fully understand why matters are escalated.

3

STRICTLY POSITIVE BEHAVIOUR MANAGEMENT

So, the Strictly Positive Teacher has nailed the relationship-building preparation necessary for behaviour management, but that's not the whole story. Now they need consciously to create the conditions to ensure good classroom management and implement a clear, consistent, easily understandable set of rules and routines to ensure that their l essons proceed smoothly and the students are able to concentrate on learning effectively.

Remember, our aim is to ensure that students' mental health and well-being are cared for, as well as our own. We want to look for good rather than bad and encourage students to *want* to behave well. In seeking to manage behaviour we want to enable students to make the right choices and, when they get things wrong, to help them address their behaviour, and then set them up to make the right choices next time. Again and again, if necessary.

This is the area in which poor or negligent practice can seriously impact on not only students' mental health, but also on the well-being of the teacher. It is a crucial part of the teacher's skill-set, and arguably the easiest to get wrong.

There are many, many factors that will affect behaviour management, and much that can be done before you ever greet the first student. The good news is that you can refine and improve your classroom-management techniques over time and you will lose nothing by continuing to try. Just as you can learn to like students, they can learn to respect and like a teacher.

❖ Planning for behaviour

There is much you can do before you even welcome your first students through the door.

First, let's look at how you create the environment for positive behaviour management before your students arrive.

Look at the classroom, not as it is but as it ought to be. If you are lucky enough to have your own classroom, all of this can be applied with ease. If you have to trail around the school with your sad box of belongings then it's more difficult, but there are still elements you can apply.

- *Your desk needs to be strategically placed so you can see, and be seen by, all pupils. It should be tidy, if possible. If, like me, you're someone whose desk can go from tidy to ridiculous in 24 hours, timetable 20 minutes a week to sort it out.*
- *Ensure that you can easily get to a board you can write on, a whiteboard or an interactive whiteboard (IWB), which the students can all see, even if they have to turn around in their seats.*
- *Arrange students' desks and chairs so that you can teach in the way you teach, whether that be in rows, groups or a horseshoe. It has to be right for you. Look at laying things out in such a way that you can easily change things around if you want to surprise your students, or teach in a different way, or just generally shake things up. Disrupting the physical environment is a very positive way of marking your territory. Changing the desk layout or changing seating plans is assertive and emphasises that this is your environment. Don't be afraid to do this within a lesson in someone else's classroom. Afterwards, you can always get a couple of kids to help you push everything back to where it was.*
- *Ensure that you can easily get to any student in the class, either to help them academically or, by function of your presence, to help them to behave. It goes without saying that the classroom must be easy to evacuate in the case of a fire drill or similar.*
- *If possible, keep one "time in" desk and chair on its own, ready in case you need to separate a student from the rest of the class. For reasons which will become apparent later when I talk about Attachment Disorder, I believe it is really important to try "time*

in" rather than "time out". (Many students who have difficulty conforming to the expectations of a classroom teacher are exhibiting behaviour borne of trauma, and there are some simple techniques teachers can employ to help lessen the effects of the trauma and thereby address the behaviour.) It may become unavoidable to remove the student later, but that is an escalation issue. Ideally, this table and chair face the wall. Ideally, there will be space nearby for an LSA, should the student need someone to help them. This desk must be kept clutter-free and available at all times. You don't want to be having to clear it when you need to use it.

- *Maintain display, relevant to what students are doing in class, and include examples, preferably with marking, of students' work. Change it regularly. I recognise that this is a counsel of perfection, and on that endless to-do list it is definitely in the "important but not urgent" category. However, if you want to get students to look at display, it has to be changed regularly.*

- *Ensure the space is kept tidy and litter-free. One of the early routines you set up could be to ensure that, at the end of every lesson once your class is waiting to be dismissed, you get them to pick up and dispose of any litter around their work-space before anyone leaves the room. (If you are a stickler for neatness, and to prevent things deteriorating quickly, you could clean the desks with graffiti cleaner at the beginning of the term and then quickly check after each lesson for a couple of days to check that no one has written on the desk; if they have, photograph it, and send the image to the child, copying the adult responsible for them in school, with the sanction you have imposed for the misdeed. It may sound pernickety and inconvenient, but you only have to do it for a week or so for the kids to get the message.)*

- *Have spare paper, pencils, pens and rulers. You shouldn't have to supply them, but in practice it will hinder the smooth flow of your lessons if you don't have them. Either make them desperately unattractive to pinch, or label them clearly with your name or classroom number. (I use the old chestnut of taking a shoe in return for a pen or pencil. It has comic value and it works! Others take mobile phones. It just has to be something that the student would never leave behind.)*

Have a couple of props for your teaching available if that's the kind of thing that floats your boat:

- *Using a ball which you throw when you ask a question and which they throw back when they answer is handy, especially in those first few lessons when you haven't fully mastered the names, but don't use one if you're a terrible thrower or catcher, and choose the ball carefully; you don't want it bouncing all over the place. As I write (in 2019), a Koosh ball is good.*
- *Also good when you're not confident of names are lolly sticks. Their use does involve quite a lot of preparation, but you use them for a whole year and it is a good way of learning those names. At the end of the year you can recycle them in a responsible way, which is a bonus.*
- *Some kind of buzzer or horn is a good way of heralding success. A student can be assigned to write names up when the teacher sounds the horn. This is a good way of keeping everyone involved and also helps you to remember names.*
- *A bell to ring when you want silence is very attractive to children. I have a service bell, the type you see on hotel reception counters. It has the benefit of only ringing if you tap it very gently. Children will ask to be the one who has the bell, and this is a reward. When you want everyone to be silent you gesture to the bell-keeper, who will ring it carefully. This is especially good when you have that end-of-term sore throat which is threatening to wreck your voice for the holidays!*

❖ Have high expectations of behaviour

Most teachers will set out their expectations when they first meet a class. Quite often these expectations will include a detailed analysis of what will happen when things go wrong. Most teachers, and schools, have a very clear sanctions ladder, starting with verbal warnings and going through detentions of various levels, maybe exclusions from classrooms, being "parked" in another classroom, up to temporary and then permanent exclusion. Obviously, the classroom teacher doesn't have to deal with the draconian end of this ladder, but the message is clear: we have numerous ways of dealing with you when you get something wrong.

Less clear, though, is the way in which we deal with those who are getting it right. The sanction-reward axis is something which, in my experience, is hotly debated in many staff rooms. There are those who assert that doing well is its own reward after all, and the expected norm is that students will cooperate in class, will do as they are asked, will work hard, give in good work, labour assiduously at their homework and hand it in with pride, secure in the knowledge that they have done their best. They will do this because they understand the relevance of education and know why they are in school, and what they get out of a formal education in the context of the whole of their lives. If they do well at school they can choose the exam options which suit them at secondary school; thereafter, their hard work will gain them access to tertiary education in a good provider, whence they will go, with their excellent grades, to a rewarding and/or financially advantageous career and a good future for their families, a comfortable home, great holidays, etc.

In my opinion this attitude is the reason that, whatever the token economy in your school, be it merits, credits, house points or whatever, the tokens are normally awarded disproportionately to those who are generally ill-behaved, in order to bribe them, or in gratitude for a brief blaze of cooperation or the handing in of mediocre, but at least completed, work. Many more able or cooperative students in many schools accept this with resignation and they and their parents, while feeling a little hard done by, will watch these other students accepting awards and cups while they are overlooked. Those who come from a healthy background with what Louise Bombér calls "good enough" parenting or caring will accept it, being able to see that working hard and doing well at school will lead probably to good outcomes and enhanced chances of success in life. Many of the young people in our care will accept this truism and will put up with being largely ignored while the miscreants are bribed with hard and soft rewards. They know they are on the way to somewhere in their future and that doing well will get them there. Amongst themselves, though, they will roll their eyes and feel slightly hard done by.

I think this is wrong on two counts. First, if it is done too obviously these "rewards" become almost a stigma in the eyes of the other students – a compensation for being naughty or weak; many students showered with inappropriate rewards will be embarrassed and the whole token economy loses any value. And second, real effort and achievement should be equally recognised. Students who do well *considering their starting point* should be rewarded. We all know what achievement looks like. If we don't acknowledge it where we see it, a proportion of those students who do well for the sake of it will not try as hard as they could, so that they only do well in the context of the class, and not in relation to their own individual abilities.

A report by the National Association for Able Children in Education (NACE) in 2007 about educating gifted children includes in its summary of findings that to raise the achievement of gifted and talented students, good schools "provide opportunities that will allow all learners to discover their potentials" and "celebrate and give equal status to all learners' potentials and achievements across the curriculum". Gifted and talented students whose achievements are not actively recognised may become disaffected and start to wonder what the point is in aiming above "good enough". The knock-on effect in schools might be that those GCSE results don't look as impressive as they might otherwise do; the effect on students might be that they underachieve.

We can see that across the population of most classrooms students need recognition of what they are doing and of their efforts and achievements. They want, or even need, to be noticed. There will be a sizeable minority of students who need attention. Lots of attention. That sanction ladder looks like a whole truckload of attention.

Being shouted at publicly may actually feel to a traumatised child like what they need. So negative attention, provoked by their behaviour, is useful in meeting their own needs. Negative response to that negative behaviour will only provoke more negative behaviour.

If the sanction ladder is not offset by a reward ladder or an alternative source of attention, then it'll do, and teachers will see negative behaviour which requires addressing.

If we accept, as pragmatic adults, that we cannot change anybody's behaviour except our own, then it is sensible to think about how we can modify our own classroom practice in order to ensure that what we see in the classroom is positive behaviour.

I must emphasise that not all students will behave in the same way, whatever expectations the teacher conveys. There are children in our schools whose pasts have traumatised them to a greater or lesser degree and made them wary of and resistant to your imposed classroom rules and expectations. You may need to accommodate those children in your classroom, and may need to adapt your rules and expectations. However, in most cases all that is necessary is to adhere carefully to the positive side of your behaviour management, and students will respond. Positive attention can be particularly effective with students who are used to a lot of negative treatment. Positive expectations of behaviour and achievement, reasonably and helpfully expressed, can also be very powerful in this context.

It is therefore a wise teacher who sets out ways in which students can get positive attention and subsequent rewards in their classroom. Multiple ways. Creative ways. Enjoyable ways.

I'm not going to pretend it's easy from the off. It requires a fundamental shift in attitude and it is hard work to master the techniques. But once you have mastered them, and their use becomes regular and normal, your classroom will become Strictly Positive, and you'll never go back.

Negative response: *"Oh, for goodness' sake! You still haven't opened your book! Why can't you follow instructions? How many times do I have to tell you... No, there's no point in arguing... Listen – who's in charge here? THAT'S ENOUGH!"*

Positive response*: "Well done! You've got your coat off already and you're in your seat. Now let's get your date and title down in your book ready for the lesson... Thank you."*

❖ Have clear rules and routines for behaviour in classrooms

Any school will have some basic routines for the beginning and end of a lesson, and this will depend on many different factors, such as the configuration of the buildings and the classrooms, the capacity of the corridors and the general climate of behaviour in the school.

Classroom teachers will create their own routines within these expectations, and a degree of individuality of approach within the guidelines is desirable.

Think about:
    a. *How you manage the entry to the classroom*
    b. *How you manage behaviour within the classroom*
    c. *How you manage the exit*

Or, in other words:
    a. *Get them in*
    b. *Get on with it and get on with them*
    c. *Get them out*

...which was the first pithy piece of advice I was ever given as a new teacher.

Some easy wins at the door

As every teacher knows, your behaviour management starts at the moment your students see you.

Particularly important are the routines you set at the classroom door. It goes without saying that every lesson is a clean sheet as far as behaviour management is concerned. Whatever happened in the last lesson, however badly Hamza or Becky behaved, they are greeted here with a warm smile that says: "I'm pleased to see you – let's make this a good lesson."

Students don't arrive at your door bright-eyed and bushy-tailed, eager for the spark of learning to be ignited into a flame. They get there hot and sweaty from PE or lunchtime football, redolent of Lynx to mask the smell, or angry because they've been excluded from a discussion about a party which will be happening this weekend, or worried about their mum's cancer, or pissed off that they haven't been able to finish the level of the game they started about 30 seconds after you should have opened the door, or in the middle of some really interesting gossip...

So. How do you create the framework? You can get some easy wins at the door, at the threshold to our territory.

- Work on those relationships. *As students are gathering, take advantage of the chance to have a word with them. Smile. Mention the match or concert they played in, or their great new haircut, or ask if they're better after they were away sick last time. Comment on their excellent book work last time, or test result, or recent improvement. Or just ask if they're okay and give them a thumbs-up and a smile. Include the potentially difficult student, perhaps encouraging them to have a good lesson with you, but be sure not to moan about the last lesson – this is a new day, a new lesson. Don't only talk to the potentially difficult ones; sprinkle your goodwill liberally. You are signalling that you are interested in the students outside your classroom, and introducing them to the lesson with positive engagement, at least with you yourself. You don't have to talk to everyone every time, but make sure that over a series of lessons no one is excluded.*
- Meet and greet. *If you don't want to be quite as chummy as that, and if you have the luxury of space in which to get your kids to line up outside, use it. Impose your expectations at the doorway. At the very least, have the class quiet outside, and greet them individually at the door. Insist on their responding to your greeting. If they walk past you without acknowledgment, ask them politely but firmly to go to the back of the queue. By doing so you are signalling the nature of your relationship. You will be polite to one another, but you are in charge.*
- Shake hands. Paul Dix of Pivotal Education advocates a school-wide approach of hand-shaking, especially at the classroom door, to ensure one-to-one civility and kindness. As a classroom teacher you could greet every child personally with a handshake at the door, which goes further and adds an element not only of formality, but added trust. Doug Lemov, American author of Teach Like a Champion, and Teach Like a Champion 2.0, alludes to this as a very basic routine for entry to a classroom. I adopted this some time ago, and I wouldn't go back. (I advise a regime of anti-bacterial hand gel twice a lesson if you do this – I won't go into why. Try not to be seen applying it! One year 7 girl spotted me applying it and was very outraged…)

Many teachers who use this routine find it very useful and observe that it improves punctuality. You could even be like American Barry White Jr, a 5th grade teacher from Charlotte, North Carolina, whose threshold routine has been watched by millions since a video was posted showing him deploying the various complex handshakes he has devised with every student in his class before they enter the room. Look him up on YouTube. How incredibly valued must those kids feel, even the girl who has chosen the really short handshake. And he says he does this every day with 60 students! They stop him in the dinner hall or in the yard to do their handshakes…

- Narrate the expected behaviour. As they are settling down, be explicit about expectations: "I'm looking for everyone to have their books out, phones away in your bags, writing down the title, date and objective, and then doing the puzzle on the board (or whatever you have chosen as your 'bell work') while you wait for the register." No negatives, only positives. "Thank you for making the start to the lesson so positive." Don't tell them what NOT to do; tell them what you expect to happen. Remember your neuro-linguistic programming truth: children focus on what you say, whether or not it is preceded by a negative.

- Entry instructions. Once the class is silent outside, give directions for what they must do when they enter the room. This may be as simple as saying, "Come in quietly, get out your books and write down the title, date and learning objective," or explaining the starter exercise you have set, which they must do after they have written down the title, date and learning objective. You are signalling that the lesson begins now, before they enter the room, and your authority starts now too. Don't expect to have to say this just once. There is no way on earth that all will remember and react appropriately. Repeat it like a mantra.

- Entry pass. *Once your class is silent outside, give them a very simple task, something which recaps what happened in the previous lesson in a simple response, which they must give in order to gain entry to the room: keywords, simple vocabulary or utterances, great synonyms for "good" – something simple. If they get to you and haven't got anything to say, they go to the back of the queue. You are signalling that your lessons are planned, and one leads to another. You are also refocussing them from History, or German, or PE and setting the mood for your subject.*

And at the other end of the lesson…

- Exit pass. *If possible, dismiss individuals at the door with a smile. You could ask them to tell you one thing they learned in your lesson which they didn't know before they came in.*
- *Stop a couple to tell them how well they did.*
- *Smile.*
- *Leave students with a positive memory of your lesson and of you; and let those you cannot praise today see how easily they could be recognised in the same way.*

❖ Manage classes effectively, using approaches that are appropriate to pupils' needs in order to involve and motivate them

Strictly Positive Behaviour Management is absolutely the heart of Strictly Positive Teaching, and is the starting point of the philosophy. SPT harnesses children's attention-seeking behaviour to lead them to *positive* behaviour, effort or work. Teachers look for *positive* behaviour, effort or work.

The basic rules are:
- *Be vigilant that no positive effort, achievement or behaviour goes unrewarded*
- *Students can only get attention for positive behaviour or activity*
- *Praise is public, specific and leads to reward*
- *Negative interaction is private, specific and leads to sanction*

So how does that work in practice?

You need to be able to record students' achievements as they occur, in real time, to show that you are noticing and valuing students' good work, behaviour and attitude. If you teach a subject where you don't have access to a board, or if you teach a practical subject where you can't always be writing things on boards, this can be effected using websites and apps, such as ClassDojo. You really only need to have access to somewhere you can write names in two lists. This could be a whiteboard you can write on and, ideally, it will be positioned where all your students can see it.

You draw a smiley face, or a "+", on one side of the board. On the other, you draw a sad face, or a "-". These symbols must be separated by the majority of the board. You will record the good deeds, effort or work on one side, and the omissions or negatives on the other. *Do not give them equal space.* There should *never* be a time when the negatives outweigh the positives, because that is not the way a class works. Remember – in 9P, 23 out of 30 students are *doing the right thing* most of the time.

When you first meet a class

As the class comes in, look for the first person to sit down, get out their pencil case and wait quietly. Ask them their name and write it up, narrating why.

"Well done, Sam. First to get ready for learning."

Now the board looks like this:

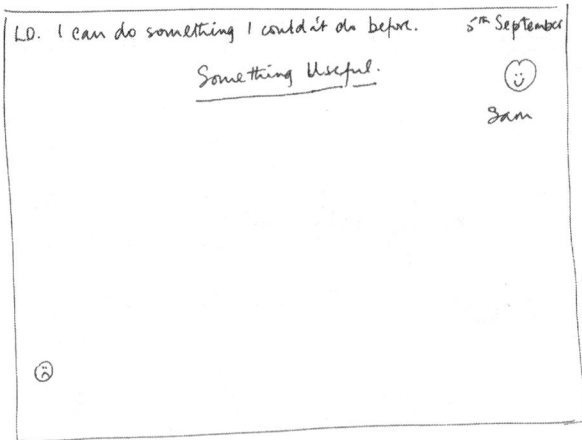

Ask the students to guess why you have added Sam's name. Several students will start to call out. When Jordan raises a hand and waits quietly to be called upon, you will ask for his name.

"Jordan – excellent. Thanks for waiting to be called upon." You add Jordan's name.

Jordan explained that Sam has done something good, so Sam's name is written under the smiley face. You add a tick for Jordan.

"Well done, Jordan! You understood that very quickly!"

Now the board looks like this:

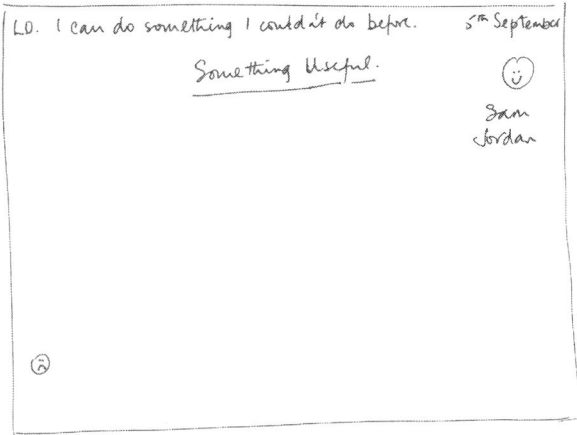

Once everyone has settled down, and after waiting for silence, you explain to the class how this is going to work.

"I've put the smiley face (or plus sign) at the top here, because I expect to have to use lots of space noting all the great things you do. The sad face (or minus sign) is set low down here because I won't need to use it much.

"Each time you do something that impresses me, I'll put your name up here. Any other thing will earn you a tick. If your name has two ticks against it, you definitely get a merit/credit/house point/etc. But sometimes something will be so good that it automatically gets a merit/credit/house point/etc on its own."

You move across to the other side.

"If anyone does something which stops me from teaching, or stops any member of the class from learning, including yourself, I will put your name here. I will not say your name – it's up to you to notice. That is your warning. If you continue that poor behaviour, I will add a tick. That is the first level sanction. If you continue again, I will add another tick; that is a second-level sanction. I am confident we won't need to do that very often."

And then in the next few minutes, you will ensure that several students get their name on the positive side of the board. Each time you narrate the reason *why* their name is going on the board, and this narration must be something specific.

"Kitty, that's a really good definition."

"Tom, well done on choosing exactly the right adjective there."

"Jasper, what an interesting thought!"

"Nabil, first to finish that task and you've done it really well."

"Amirah, thank you for helping out Ellie."

"Ellie, well done for noticing that I'd made a mistake – now the others won't copy it down wrong."

In that first lesson, try *not* to get any negative names on the board. At the end of the lesson, the board looks like this, and you run through it and give all the named individuals their reward. Make sure you add all the promised points to your school management system; it is essential that students feel they can trust you to follow through on your promises.

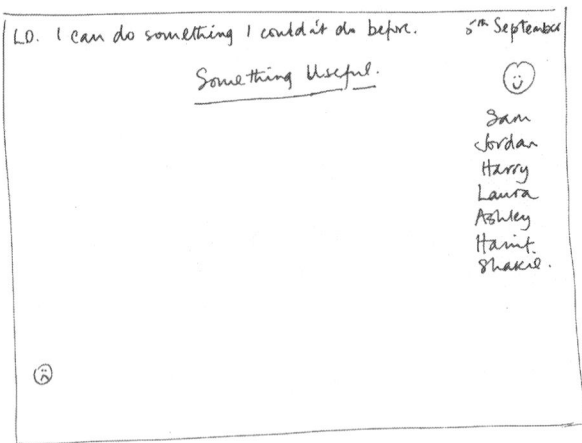

The rules will be recapped at the start of all of the next few lessons. Once the class settles into a routine, there will come a point where you will need to put a name on the negative side of the board without saying the name.

When this happens, the named person will question why their name is on the board, because they have already forgotten the rules. Choose a phrase to use in this situation. For example:

"I'm not having a conversation about that now. See me at the end of the lesson."

If they query it again, add a tick to their name. This is a first-level sanction. Try not to look at them but carry on the lesson and, as quickly as possible, find someone to commend, verbally, while putting their name on the other side of the board. The message is clear: if you want my attention, do something positive.

In this early lesson if the poor behaviour continues, specify: "I am not interrupting the teaching and learning in my classroom to discuss negatives with you. See me at the end of the lesson." Add a second tick, which indicates a second-level sanction. If they persist, they will have to be removed.

After a few lessons you won't need to recap the rules any more for most of the students. Most students will understand the system. As you get to know your students better you'll find there are some (those who have specific learning difficulties such as an autistic spectrum disorder, for instance) who need a regular recap of the system; with some students you might even have to do a one-minute recap before every single lesson in order for them to remember it. But it is essential that all students know exactly what it is you're doing and why. They need to know there will be consistency, both on the praise and the sanction side of the system. They will know it is predictable and fair.

If a teacher has judged it correctly, when there is a buzz of low-level disruption, all they will need to do is move over to the negative side of the board with their dry-board pen, take the lid off and look around to see whose name will go up first, and the buzz will magically subside.

When that first student gets two ticks and has to stay behind after class, they are without an audience and, generally, anxious to leave. Indicate their name on the board and explain to them that, given their behaviour, you could not have done anything else. You might enumerate the stages that led to this or you may not, dependent on circumstances. This will be down to the individual student; some students who have specific conditions may need to have things explained more carefully to them before they understand. And it is very important that they do understand the sanction, and also understand how to avoid one next time. Next time you will greet them warmly and then do your best to find some positive behaviour, effort or work to commend early in the lesson.

There are some students whose presence will mean that their class will need a quick recap at the beginning of every lesson.

That is Strictly Positive Behaviour Management in a nutshell. But let's take a little time to review those rules.

1. *Be vigilant that no positive effort, achievement or behaviour goes unrewarded*

   Paul Dix, in his excellent book When the Adults Change, Everything Changes, calls the negative form of this, where the names of miscreants are scratched angrily on the board by an irate teacher, "naming and faming", as opposed to "naming and shaming". I think he is absolutely right in this; however it doesn't take much of a flip to turn "naming and faming" into a very positive thing! There is always good stuff to notice if you are vigilant, just as you can always find something to criticise if you look for it.

   The key here is that it may be minor, but whatever is rewarded must be real. There must be a valid exchange – a proper positive effort for a word of encouragement. And these are personal as well as public exchanges.

   There are some students for whom a reward for having a pen is valid – that student who almost never has a pen, and always has to be lent one, leading to a delay in the start of a lesson. If they appear with a pen and write down the date straight away, then it is perfectly valid to say "Mohammed! You've brought your pen! I think you definitely get your name on the board!" The other students will understand why this is marked with praise, because they know that he often doesn't have a pen. If you were to praise Hassan, who always has a pen, for having a pen, that would be obviously invalid. Hassan needs to identify an infinitive in a German sentence to get his name on the board.

If Stacey from 9P comes in, scowling but without argument, gets her book and pen out and settles down straight away, you might catch her eye, smile and put her name on the board as you heave a sigh of relief that you've not been pitched into a fruitless argument before your lesson has even started. The rest of the class will understand why she has been given a reward, and most are probably as relieved as you are.

Praise as a reward should be specific, spontaneous and genuine, and should focus on some attribute of work or behaviour, rather than a quality of the individual student. No exclaiming at someone's cleverness as you write their name up, or their creativity, but the remembering of a rule introduced and applied a few lessons ago, or the creation of an interesting sentence using vocabulary introduced in a different context. It is well known that part of nurturing a growth mindset is implanting the idea that intelligence is malleable, and a teacher does that by praising a student's effort and deeds rather than their talent.

That doesn't mean intrinsic qualities shouldn't, in some circumstances, be rewarded. On occasion such praise can be memorable for students, but that should be in the form of a personal conversation. After all, if you tell someone in the full class setting that they show enormous resilience, you are conveying all sorts of other knowledge about that individual which is probably inappropriate in public.

Let's take a minute to discuss "reward"
Every student wants to feel that their teachers like them and think they are doing well. Anything teachers do which makes a student feel they have done well is a reward.

This can be as simple as a private smile or a gesture; it can be accompanied by a word or a phrase; it can take the form of a name written up on a board. All of these will make a student feel good about themselves and what they are doing. Generally, the quieter and less demanding a student is, the happier they will be with the discreet end of this spectrum.

Schools tend to be token economies and rewards can take the form of credits/merits/house points or similar, the accumulation of which can lead to more concrete rewards such as "golden time", social rewards, vouchers or even money. These are always useful, especially when they build a sense of competition and/or community where some groups will measure up against other groups. Teachers must beware, however, that such tokens don't become devalued by becoming compensation for the less academic students, or placebos for disruptive or challenging students. Those quiet, cooperative students who make up the majority of 9P must not be penalised for their quietness, cooperation… ordinariness. Teachers should be vigilant for opportunities to praise the work of these students, too. Those totals read out at the end of term in the celebration assembly should not be an embarrassing roster of all the weakest or most difficult students. The high achievers and the "ordinary" students should be appropriately represented.

Stickers and stamps are great, but their use must be consistent, at least within a class. Students will read great meaning into a casually used stamp, and will notice when suddenly it ceases to appear. And stickers are quite an investment if teachers buy them out of their own purse! Perhaps they should be saved for very, very special work.

Then there are sweets and chocolate and other hard rewards. While students love edible rewards and will work for them, they can be perceived as bribes rather than proper rewards. If they are not available, the work may not be forthcoming, and if the work has been done and there is no chocolate proffered in return, then students can become most disgruntled and feel cheated. Again, these can be a major drain on a teacher's finances, and maybe they should be reserved for ends of term as a celebratory form of praise. Otherwise, there is a risk that the absence of such hard rewards, when they come, renders the soft rewards meaningless in some students' eyes.

2. *Students can only get attention for positive behaviour or activity*
Okay, I'm going to admit it – this is really difficult, even when you've been doing it for years. The temptation to express frustration at the same negative behaviour a student manifests time and again in your classroom can be almost overwhelming. This is especially the case when you're trying to put these strategies into place. However, it really is worth trying again and again and again until it starts to become habit forming. It really does work. If you stick rigorously to

commenting on or narrating positives, those tricky attention-seeking students will eventually come around.

It is almost impossible not to lapse occasionally into a slightly whiny, moany moment in the face of poor behaviour in your classroom, but luckily it is relatively easy to change tack and become Strictly Positive. You do this simply by catching yourself being negative and redressing the balance to seek out positives, name them, and then take it from there.

Zac is a tricky character. Bright but challenging, he could do the work, but prefers to make the class laugh. You are questioning the class and he puts up his hand. "Great!" you think. You call upon him and he gives you an irrelevant comedic answer. The temptation is to tell him how pointless it is and make him the cynosure of all eyes. If you do this, he has achieved his objective. Instead, you completely ignore his response and call upon someone else, applauding their contribution (if it merits it) and writing their name up positively. When you have a chance you can write Zac up negatively without a word. He'll know why. If you ignore him, he may well volunteer again, this time with a sensible answer. At this stage you write his name up, describing the positives.

Zena will not work unless someone prompts her to do so. Her key worker is off sick and she doesn't start when you set a task, despite you checking in with her at the beginning of the task and making sure she knew what to do. You are aware of her not doing the work so you comment quietly to her that she hasn't done the work and write her name up. Then you go into nag mode and she racks up two negative ticks in quick succession. You are now obsessed with her lack of work. Her name is on the board, yes – she has already got a detention – but she still hasn't started. But then you think… actually, I broke my own rule. I whined at her, by name, each time I wrote her name on the board or added a tick. Her neighbour was working really well, but I didn't exclaim at her work and write her name up on the positive side – I was blindsided by the omissions. What I should have done was look around her for people to praise (specifically…) and name them frequently. I could then have glanced without comment at her empty page. If she started I should then have named her and written up her name (remember: this is a real achievement – she doesn't usually work independently on her own).

3. Praise is public, specific and leads to reward

The rewards are your gifts to the child for doing well. A word of praise is a reward, as is a smile or a simple recognition of something they didn't know you'd noticed. ("You've been putting your hand up more this week – well done!") But there are many options available to you. Most schools have limited rewards available to them, as we have noted previously.

However, there are always ways in which you can work with a child to ensure you tailor their rewards to them. Some schools or departments will provide a menu of rewards from which children can select an option. These might include, for instance:

o *A phone call or email, to whomever they want you to contact, is always welcome. Asking is good: a student who receives close supervision from a particular senior leader or the SENCo may want them to know that they've had a great lesson in your class – it may mitigate some of the trouble they're in elsewhere in the school! Most students will ask you to contact home, and they prefer a phone call because it's more immediate and they will get feedback as soon as they get home.*

o *Recently, wanting to single out exceptional achievement or behaviour from the merely good, I started a "best seat in the house" initiative in addition to the normal token rewards. The student who's had the most successful lesson can choose a friend and they will sit in the "best seats in the house" in the next lesson. These seats are equipped with a massive set of colouring pens, rubbers, stencil rulers, pencils and pens. The seats come with the privilege of drinking your own drinks. The colouring pens are the real draw! Usually it's the teacher who selects this one individual, but you might like to ask the students who they think has done the best – sometimes they can be remarkably insightful.*

o *Students may get a pass to sit with a friend in the next lesson*

o *Tickets for a raffle can also be good*

- *One teacher I know offers cups of tea as rewards for older students!*

It is definitely the case that schools could be more imaginative about rewards, especially as students get older. As any parent of a later teenage child knows, the desire to be rewarded and praised does not go away as you reach 16 or even 18. In fact, most adults – including me – enjoy being told explicitly that they are doing a good job.

4. Negative interaction is private, specific and leads to sanctions

There is a key truth here, and that is that students are much keener to have a lengthy conversation with a teacher about their behaviour when they have a large audience and when it's taking up teaching and learning minutes, than when their audience has left the room and they are taking up their own time. Any conversation you have with a child about their negative behaviour within the context of a lesson is being conducted on their terms. The conversation you have after the class has left is on your terms.

So, as the class has left you can indicate the board and check that the student understands what sanction they have incurred and how they incurred it. You can ensure they know that they left you with no room for manoeuvre and that in order to be fair you had *to award that sanction. They need to know that they* earned *this sanction – you did not choose it for them. This must be crystal clear. They earned the sanction and it stands in exactly the same way that* if they earned a reward *then that, too, must stand and cannot be taken away from them.*

Then you may, if it's appropriate, choose to find something you can change in order to help them avoid similar sanctions in future lessons. This may be a change in the seating plan, an agreement that you will devise a prompt between you – a tap on the desk perhaps, or a gesture – which might indicate they are in danger of receiving a sanction, or perhaps some form of scaffolding support for the work in the next lesson. This shows you want to help. You are turning a negative into a positive.

This conversation should be brisk, taking no more than a couple of minutes. Whatever you do, don't moan or rant or make it personal. The student probably has another lesson to get to, or lunch. When they have gone, thinking now about the offer of help rather than the sanction, you hope, make a quick note about your agreement and stick to it.

❖ **Establish a framework for discipline with a range of strategies, using praise, sanctions and rewards consistently and fairly.**

Specific Praise and Specific Sanctions

In many classrooms, were you a fly on the wall, you might witness a scene that goes something like this:

Teacher: *"Who threw that paper? It was you, Joe, wasn't it?"*

Joe: *"No it wasn't! Why are you picking on me? You always pick on me! I didn't do anything!"*

Teacher: *"Yes, you did! I saw you! You actually ripped a page out of your book... look here! You can even see where you ripped it out! Look! Joe – I'm telling you to look! Then I saw you scrunch it up and throw it at Tom... And there's no point looking like that, Tom... You're just as bad..."*

Tom and Joe gesticulate to indicate their total innocence and the unreasonableness of their teacher. All eyes are on them.

Meanwhile the rest of the class put down their pens and wait patiently for the scene to play out.

Later in the same lesson:

Max makes an excellent point.

Teacher: *"Yes, Max. Well done! Excellent!"*

Teacher moves on to the next student, who also offers a useful insight.

"Good job, Louis! Brilliant!"

Which looks more important? The tearing out and throwing of the paper, or the excellent academic response to the teaching? Who gets more attention in that class? Joe or Max? How are Joe and Max going to feel at the end of this?

Let's replay that scenario in the classroom of a Strictly Positive Teacher.

Teacher spots the page being torn out and thrown across the room. He scoops it up without comment and drops it in the bin. He walks over to the board and writes Joe's name, in the bottom left-shand corner under the ☹, placed discreetly, low down on the board, for this precise purpose before the students walked through the door.

Joe knows not to argue. If he protests, the sanction he has earned will be increased. He needs to stay behind after the lesson for a quick chat. If he doesn't, his sanction will again be increased.

As the teacher finishes his teaching point, he asks a question.

Max answers.

Teacher: *"An excellent response, Max. You've made a good point about... And you also noticed... You also expressed yourself very well – I like the use of the keyword _____."*

Teacher goes to the board and adds Max's name to a long list that covers most of the right-hand side of the board under the ☺, which was drawn on the top right of the board before the class arrived.

What's more important here? The tearing out and throwing of the paper, or the excellent academic response to the teaching? Who gets more attention in that class? Joe or Max? How are Joe and Max going to feel at the end of this?

In the Strictly Positive classroom the focus is on what matters, and what matters is the positive learning and behaviour that is happening in the classroom. Nothing negative should be allowed to become the focus, but negative behaviour should nevertheless be dealt with strictly and firmly.

This emphatically does *not* mean you shower students with unfocussed and meaningless praise.

There are many versions found online of advice to teachers on how to praise students along these lines:

Pointless Praise #1.
- Good work!
- Well done!
- You champion!
- Thank you so much!
- Nice job!
- You're a legend!
- You are awesome!
- That's awesome!
- fantastic!

Here's another one:

Pointless Praise #2

All very well, I suppose, as long as you don't mind your students feeling patronised and greeting these utterances with an inward sneer.

Students aren't idiots, and they can spot a patronising teacher a mile off. At best, such platitudes will have zero effect, showing, as they do, that you're not really paying attention to what they're saying or doing. At worst, it will make them resistant to you and any opinion you express.

To have any weight, praise must be specific and focussed on what the student is doing and the effort they're making. By contrast, notice poor behaviour visually but not verbally: reserve negative interaction for a conversation after the class, so as not to interrupt teaching and learning, and ensure it's clear what sanction it attracts.

Praise and noticing what a student has done right is often also a useful preliminary to asking them to do something else. Someone is much more likely to want to do something you ask if what they have done right has been appreciated – a verbal three stars and a wish; that is simple human nature and not confined to dealing with young people.

Negative (or false positive) response:

"Good."

"Yes."

"Well done."

"Yes, great. But you haven't underlined your title."

Positive response:

"You pronounced that really well."

"Great – you've used two keywords in that response."

"You stepped up to the challenge – correct use of pathetic fallacy."

"Great – your presentation is better than it usually is; nice clear handwriting, and you've already made a start on the exercise. Now I just need you to underline the title."

Body language and positioning

Part of being positive is having a positive awareness of how everything we do has an impact on everyone we encounter, not least the children whom we teach.

How you position yourself in relation to the class and the students communicates powerful messages. Usually these messages are communicated subliminally, but why not be aware of ways in which you can communicate through your physical position? One of the primary goals of Strictly Positive Teaching is to build better relationships between students and teachers. Your physical presence in the classroom will be a big contributor to this and may help with behaviour management.

You as the teacher will usually be the focus of attention in the classroom for most of your students for at least some of the time. Each teacher has their own "presence" and this will vary hugely from professional to professional. However, one thing is true: you can change the impact of your presence, and therefore what you communicate to students, by the way you position yourself and hold yourself in the classroom. You can assert your presence by being obvious to them all, and you can withdraw subtly to enable other activities to take place as you observe them.

Although it may be counter-intuitive, teachers have to be positively aware that every time we change position – standing, sitting, leaning, crouching, facing, beside or behind a student – we send out complex messages and influence the way our students behave. If you think about it too much it might feel as if you're behaving like Cato, from *The Pink Panther* films, always ready to appear from nowhere...

Our choice of position will depend on a number of factors:
- *The activity which is in progress*
- *Where we want the focus of the student to be*
- *How the groupings in the room are working*
- *The "feel" of the lesson*
- *The age of the learners*
- *The usual behaviour of the learners*

Let's look at what you are communicating without meaning to as you roam your territory:

STANDING

Adopting a standing position indicates that you are taking control. You are at a different level from the students; they can all see you and you can see them. You can therefore command, physically and verbally, the whole room.

Whenever you wish to have the attention of the whole class it is sensible to stand. Standing completely still can have a powerful effect in quieting a group, once patterns have been established. Even better if you can make yourself bigger – by raising your arms, or putting hands on hips, for example – to attract attention (who says we can't learn from those spitting cats with their fur on end?)

I'm a short person. We have to work a bit harder than our tall colleagues on commanding our space. It is tempting to do that by combining a big voice with a small stature, but that takes a toll on your voice after a while and a loud voice, however big, ceases to have impact after a time.

Teaching from a standing position shows that you are positive and in control. It also shows you are interested. You can easily make eye contact with students, looking from one individual to the next and making sure they are looking back at you. This means that if your eye settles on something you do not wish to see – the back of someone's head, for instance – you can stop talking and wait until the head turns around. Being seated, especially at a computer, may look as if you've lost interest in the class and can have a negative effect on behaviour and engagement.

If you approach a student and retain a standing position but look over the work, you're saying to that student that you are overseeing them. This can be a fairly neutral position, but the student will usually derive the correct message. If they are working hard, they will wait for praise or comment, whereas if they are not working as they should be, your presence will probably have a positive effect on both them and their neighbours, and you will see them redirecting themselves to their work.

Changing from a seated position to standing, one increases the perception of the balance of control in the class. It's a good way to resume your place as the focus of the class. By changing position, you can change the atmosphere in the class. If you are sitting, and the class becomes too loud, standing up should make a difference, especially if you make use of non-verbal signals. Beware of standing up and yelling in an unfocussed way, which makes you seem a bit desperate, and is strangely ineffectual.

LEANING AND CROUCHING

When you lean on a table and look at students' work, you demonstrate focus on a particular group or individual but without committing to a particular course of action. You are literally looking over their work, surveying what's going on. If you lean with two hands on the table, this can be quite intimidating. In certain specific situations you may wish to be intimidating, of course; but if you don't, be aware of this.

When you shift from a leaning position to crouching down beside them, you're saying, "Okay, let me help you with this," because you're coming down to their level and making the connection an individual one. This is a great tool for working with students, especially those who are struggling in some way, but beware of remaining in this bubble too long as you are invisible to the rest of the class as a whole, and they may take advantage.

SITTING

Sitting can either positively indicate that you are relaxed, you are shifting to a cooperative working environment or, if you get it wrong, that you have a lack of interest in what's going on.

When a teacher sits behind his or her desk the students cannot see clearly what they are doing. If the teacher then sets an exercise and sits looking at their computer, the students will rightly come to the conclusion that the teacher is engaged in another activity, one which excludes them, and they may feel neglected or freed from normal teacher restraints. We've probably all heard those student complaints about the colleague who puts a task on the board and then "just answers her emails".

It is difficult to convey a sense of energy when seated. This can sometimes be of benefit. When a parent reads a bedtime story to a child they don't do it wandering upright around the room, because they want to soothe and create a cosy feeling. In the same way in certain situations it can be effective to pull a chair to the front of the class and read or explain something, or tell a story. Here, you are inviting students to concentrate on the words, rather than on your movements.

However, if you are asking a student to be the focus of the class, whether leading a starter activity, perhaps, or presenting a research project, it can be useful to remove yourself from the centre of attention and withdraw to a sitting position behind a desk.

A seated position conveys a relaxed sense, which can indicate trust. With smaller groups, if the teacher sits down at a group of tables with them, the students can feel that this is a more mature environment. They are trusted with a slightly more collegiate way of working. They may respond well to this, but if they don't prove worthy of your trust, moving the chair away and taking back control by standing for the rest of the lesson should correct any impression that you are a soft touch.

When walking around the room and looking at work, if you are able to pull up a chair and sit with a student, you are conveying a sense that you will work *with* the student to solve their problems. It says that you're giving them your time.

As with so much of what the teacher does in the classroom, your physical position helps you to manage behaviour, convey messages and support students. Varying your position can be an easy way to help you remain Strictly Positive in the classroom.

❖ Take responsibility for promoting good and courteous behaviour in classrooms

This is an incredibly important area for teachers who want their practice to be strictly positive. For whatever reason, the relationships in a classroom between teacher and students, but also between students, can take a sudden nosedive if not properly controlled. Students can fall out over something tiny and trouble can spread quickly and involve multiple others over the course of a single Geography lesson without the teacher noticing, if that teacher is not alert to the atmosphere in a room. When the teacher is not teaching from the front and the students are engaged on a writing exercise, pair work or group work, it is surprisingly easy for these situations to arise. The first hint for the teacher may be when one student dissolves into tears or storms out of your room, or actually hits another.

You can learn to read a room and spot these behaviours early. It may well be that you are aware of the volatile characters in your class, quite often the students whose behaviour you have planned for. You may also be aware of the volatile relationships in the class; maybe you have the two girls who are sometimes best friends and at other times sworn enemies. Maybe the two boys who used to be best friends but then there was a girl... or the kids who were in a romantic relationship but have now turned on each other with visceral ferocity. It is important not to be so involved with one child, group of children, or table, that you lose your overall gauge of the temperature of the room.

The best way to avoid such problems arising in your room is to be very assertive:

1. *Demand politeness from all to all as a condition of being in your classroom*
2. *Never overlook unpleasantness when it arises*
3. *Never publicly challenge the behaviour but intervene at once*
4. *Immediately move one of the students, or both*
5. *Do not engage with students about the reasons for moves*
6. *Ask both students to see you after the lesson*
7. *In a private conversation at the end, try to get students to agree*
8. *If they won't, escalate immediately*

It is also essential for a teacher to be polite to everyone in their classroom. If we don't model politeness it is difficult to demand it from our charges. It is essential to watch our language and never to make blanket personal comments, but always to ensure that any negative comment that escapes you (because we can behave less than perfectly sometimes...) is applied to behaviour rather than to character.

Recently I watched a clip on our local news of a transgender male student talking about his transition and how his school handled it. He mentioned that one teacher had mimicked his high voice, and it was clearly something that had hurt him deeply. I'm certain that teacher had no intention of upsetting him, but it's possible they were uncertain as to how to behave, and this was interpreted as cruelty.

The obvious hurt of this student struck me as powerful evidence of how one teacher's throwaway remark, gesture, or inadvertent facial expression can speak volumes to a student in a way that will stay with them for ever. It is another of those cases that illustrate how important it is to remember that you as the teacher are the adult in the room, and as such you do have to be careful of everything you say, because the students are children. Even the sixth formers are still children. Those teachers who are old enough to have children who have passed through the whole school system recognise that year 11s don't come back after two months of holiday and in their own clothes miraculously transformed into adults. As children they are still vulnerable to perceived slights or being teased by adults, especially adults who are in a position of authority. We mustn't abuse our authority and must try our best not to abuse it accidentally through carelessness.

❖ Promote good and courteous behaviour around the school, in accordance with the school's behaviour policy

In many situations a teacher is well advised to pick their battles, but wandering around the school ignoring students' transgressions can cause problems for colleagues. Schools will all have different policies and teachers should uphold these policies in a consistent fashion. If a teacher decides unilaterally that they don't think it's important to uphold the uniform policy, and blithely walks past six kids with their shirts untucked or wearing trainers, or ties undone, or lets them listen to music in class, or doesn't confiscate phones being used in class, or whatever the particular beef of the school is, then they immediately make it a personal thing when other teachers do.

"But Mr Hayman says it's okay/doesn't mind/didn't say anything!"

Thanks, Mr Hayman – you just made it difficult to hold the school line without dropping you in it, which no teacher wants to do to a colleague.

Lack of consistency is a killer to a school behaviour policy. It is possible to be weird or wacky in your own classroom while still upholding the tenets of the school policy. If students aren't allowed to listen to music, then they're not allowed to listen to music in *any* classroom, even if you think it makes your life easier and so that shouldn't be the rule. If you feel that way then take it up with the Senior Leadership team and make your case – don't let your behaviour make the lives of colleagues more difficult.

4

STRICTLY POSITIVE EXPECTATIONS

If as Strictly Positive Teachers we are seeking to teach in a way that recognises what students can do, rather than focussing on what they can't do, then clearly the area of expectation setting is really important to get right. We need to have high expectations of our young people (remember educational rule #1: *students live up or down to their teachers' expectations of them*); but, equally, we don't want to expect so much of them that the conscientious ones flog themselves to death trying to meet those high expectations, or the disengaged students give up and conclude that, as they always suspected, they are failures. It is an area that demands professional expertise, and it is an area in which teachers become more proficient as they progress in their career.

The Strictly Positive key to success in this area is to identify something in each lesson that students cannot do and try to ensure that by the end of the lesson, to a greater or lesser degree, they *can* do it. In this way, students are conscious of their own progress and achievement in a lesson, which will motivate them to succeed in future lessons.

❖ Set high expectations which inspire, motivate and challenge pupils

> *"If you treat an individual as he is, he will remain as he is. But if you treat him as if he were what he ought to be and what he could be, he will become what he ought to be and what he could be."*

It is amazing that we can look back to the late 18th century to find Johann Wolfgang von Goethe expounding on one of the absolute fundamental principles of what he would never in a million years have called Positive Teaching.

A few years ago a teacher told me proudly how he read up on students before they came into his class. Great, I thought – absolutely what you need to do. Then he told me how he would identify those students who had what he called "a chequered past" and draw them aside just before the start of his first class.

"Ryan," he would say, wagging his finger in the student's face, "I know all about you. A quick word to the wise: don't mess about in my class or I'll come down on you like a tonne of bricks."

My face fell. Before Ryan had even entered the class for his first ever lesson with Mr G, he knew what the game was. Battle lines were drawn. Game on.

Let's forget Mr G's approach and focus on what is a good starting point for establishing mutual expectations between students and teachers.

You've prepared thoroughly. Your classroom is set out as you want it, and the display is attractive and resilient, fully relevant to this unit's learning. You've researched the students – there won't be any surprises, you've tailored your seating plan to fit your recently acquired knowledge about the newcomers. You've looked at the photos on the school system and there are a few names you've taken in.

You have written your learning objective for the first lesson on the board, you've got your piles of textbooks labelled and ready to give out, your exercise books and your stampers and rewards, and you're ready!

You go to the door and, if you're lucky enough to have the space to allow it, you urge them all to get into a line. You ask for silence, and then you wait for it. When all are silent, you explain to the students that you want them to find their seat and sit down as quickly and quietly as possible.

Then, with a smile, you invite the students into the classroom. As each one passes you, you try to make eye contact and greet them, adding some small personal exchange with any students whom you already know.

You have already communicated several things:

- *You are someone with high expectations*

- *You are friendly and not suspicious of any of them*
- *You treat them like individuals*
- *You remember important things, personal things*

As those students walk in, you have a chance to make your mark.

Many teachers set out their expectations during their first lesson, and this is obviously a very good idea. However, in many cases this expectation-setting tends to take the form of a list of rules that the teacher has laid down, and is heavy on the "what happens if you don't comply" side of things. I worry about this, as it indicates an expectation that the rules you have outlined will not be adhered to. It also overlooks the expectations the students can, and should, have of the teacher.

As the students are the customers, perhaps it would be wiser to spend a little more time talking about the mutual contract, about what happens in the classroom and why, and why the way you have set things up is the way in which everyone in the class can achieve their own objectives: the teacher is able to teach effectively so that the students are able to learn effectively.

The classroom expectations in any institution are essentially very simple: the student expects to be able to learn at a pace appropriate to them, without undue disruption, able to take learning risks without fear of put-downs or humiliation; the teacher expects to be able to teach, safely, without undue disruption and able to work to each individual's best advantage. All the variations on this theme are just that.

A Strictly Positive Teacher might introduce the students' classroom expectations as follows:

- *The class will learn or practise something new or useful in every lesson*
- *The teacher will work with them to help them achieve to the fullest of their potential*
- *The teacher will encourage and motivate them*
- *The teacher will ensure that the classroom environment is conducive to learning*

(They might not use the word "conducive", but the inclusion of this last point sends out a positive message: that disruptive behaviour has no place in this environment. This is a place of learning, and the majority can expect steps to be taken to ensure that no one is permitted to spoil their learning chances.)

In the interests of ensuring that students' expectations are met, the teacher then outlines her expectations of the students. These are positively phrased to avoid any negative words.

Parents will recognise the wall/road analogy. When a parent starts walking with their tiny charge to the park, or playgroup or a playdate, the absolute terror is that the child might dart between the cars onto the road and meet a nasty fate. The parent's instinct will be to shout nervously, "Don't go onto the road!" because the road looms large in their mind. This is obviously because the risk – the road – is what they're thinking about. But small children don't hear the "don't go onto the..." in that sentence. What they hear is the key word – *ROAD*. And so they look at, and gravitate towards, the road. Much better, from a neuro-linguistic processing point of view, is to say, "Walk next to the *WALL/FENCE/GRASS,*" so that the keyword signals what they should be listening out for and thereby are directed to.

Frankly, by the time they get to secondary school, let alone primary school, they haven't changed much. In all my years I haven't evolved much either. If someone were to say to me, "You shouldn't eat pizza," all I hear is PIZZA. If you were to say instead, "You need to eat more SALAD," I can see a plate of salad. I never thought about the pizza, so the salad looks delicious.

So you can set out your expectations framed as "I" statements. We all know what they look like. They go something like this:

- *I will always do my best*
- *I will complete all work to the best of my ability*
- *I will show respect to my fellow students and my teacher*
- *I will think carefully, but I will ask for help whenever I need it*

At this stage there should be no mention of any sanctions. You are utterly confident that all will go well. There might be one slightly braver student who will put up his hand and say:

"What if we *don't* do our best or we *do* distract people?"

Of course, you should pre-plan your own response to this, which is a blatant attempt to set the teacher up in opposition to this student and, by extension, the class and thereby get some sort of vicarious control. However, I would urge you strongly not to fall into the trap of negativity. My habitual response, and one which I use in probably one out of every three encounters with a new class, is always the same. I smile broadly and look directly at the questioner and I say:

"You will."

And then I immediately turn away and talk to someone else.

One final thing: do not allow the expectation-setting administrative tasks to take up the whole of the lesson, which is admittedly difficult if you have a 35-minute lesson, but instead plan to include something which your class can say they have done in your lesson.

Then, once your students are standing in silence and have tidied up any mess that has been created, go to the door and say goodbye to each of them, one by one, meeting their eyes and smiling. Leave them with the impression of a clear and understandable classroom environment where everyone will work together to the benefit of all. This is a cooperative endeavour and we all have our part to play.

❖ Establish a safe and stimulating environment for pupils, rooted in mutual respect

Who is in charge? Own the room

> *"It is a curious thing, Harry, but perhaps those who are best suited to power are those who have never sought it. Those who, like you, have leadership thrust upon them, and take up the mantle because they must, and find to their own surprise that they wear it well."*
> Albus Dumbledore, as quoted by JK Rowling.

Contrary to all those jokes, which most of us have heard a gazillion times from acquaintances at social functions, most teachers probably didn't go into the career because they like pushing kids around, or because they thought of themselves as leaders or managers of people. They didn't think they'd have to adopt strategies to make large numbers of students do their bidding – they just wanted to teach their subject.

However, the problem is that we're not working with people who are necessarily there out of choice. Unlike soldiers, teachers or office workers, students aren't there because they have chosen a particular career, but because society has decreed that they must attend school. In addition, they are children, and children don't necessarily share your view that learning your subject in your lesson is the most important thing they have to do that day. They may not like your subject, they may not like school, they may just have had a terrible morning, a massive row with their best friend, or the elderly family tortoise may have died. Part of being strictly positive is understanding that you have therefore to assume the mantle of leadership, you have to have strategies for leadership and you have to take control.

As I mentioned under Planning for behaviour, there is a lot you can do before your students even appear in your classroom, and this starts with the basics of your relationship with your students and the space in which you teach. The very first thing you can do before you start teaching is to take positive control of the space and the classroom as a whole in order to be able to control the learning that takes place in it. If you don't do this essential piece of preparation, things can get difficult quite quickly.

1. *This is your room. It is not the students' room. Even if you have to move classrooms five times a day, the classroom in which you are teaching is, for the time that you are in it, your classroom. You decide (unless your school unwisely decrees otherwise…) when and how the students come into the classroom; you decide under what circumstances they are permitted to leave it; you decide who sits where, and if you wish them to change seating in the middle of the lesson (a strategy I heartily recommend – again, see Planning for behaviour) then they move. Don't be confined to the front of the classroom – use the whole of the space. Teach from the back. Teach from next to a*

tricky student. Teach wandering around the room. Sit on a chair at the back of the class while they are working. It's your room.

2. *This is your class. You decide where they sit. Where they sit will probably change for different reasons. Sometimes you may prefer them in mixed-ability groups. Sometimes you will want certain students to explore something which is a little more complex, so you may wish to have students grouped according to ability (or target grade, which is more diplomatic). Sometimes you may want students to do some reciprocal teaching, so may want students who are stronger in your subject paired with those who are less keen and able. Sometimes you may wish to have whole exercises that require students moving around the room. The point is – it's your decision.*

You need to be sure of this yourself. Confidence communicates itself and if students know you are in control they will go with it. Luckily, confidence can also be faked. If you actually practise using all the strategies mentioned in a) and b), you will communicate confidence to the students, and that will make you more confident as a leader.

As the old saying goes, in a completely different context: "Fake it until you make it!"

❖ Set goals which stretch and challenge pupils of all backgrounds, abilities and dispositions

Planning: giving yourself the best chance of success

Failing to plan is planning to fail

I was in business for a few years before I came into education, and I have a lot of these little aphorisms to hand. But this one is spot on. Many battles are won and lost in the planning phase, and I'm not just talking here about lesson planning. You can go a long way to ensuring Strictly Positive behaviour management before you even meet the kids you are going to teach.

Research your pupils

The people with whom we will be interacting are small people, and people are complex. Although many of us will joke that we can tell what a student is going to be like once she has been in our classroom for five minutes, what we don't know is *why* she is behaving like this. And if we don't know why she is behaving like this, it is unlikely that we will be able to help her change her behaviour.

Is she struggling to cope academically, so that she is creating an alternative persona in order to hide the fact that she feels so utterly unable to keep up with her peers, distracting the learning because she is fearful that she can't keep up?

- *Is she hungry? Does she have to fend for herself because parents are ill, asleep after a night shift, substance-addicted or frequently absent?*
- *Is she tired? Does she live in her bedroom, untroubled by family who let her stay up playing online games or chatting on social media until 3am?*
- *Does she have non-verbal reasoning scores that are through the roof, but really low language scores so that she lives her life unable to express all the complex ideas that are running around her brain?*

Read all the Special Educational Needs (SEN) reports on your new students andake sure you know who has dyslexia; dyspraxia; Social Anxiety (SA); Attention Deficit Hyperactivity Disorder (ADHD); Attachment Disorder (AD); Oppositional Defiance Disorder (ODD); an Autistic Spectrum Condition (ASC); or any other conditions or disorders. Find out who is in receipt of Pupil Premium, or entitled to free school meals, or who does not speak English at home. These are the students with whom, potentially, you will have to work to create a positive bond in these important early lessons. Work with the Learning Support Assistants and pastoral leaders; if the students have key workers, talk to them. Find a way of noting anything important discreetly in your mark book. In addition, find out who already has, or is likely to show, high skills in your subject area, and think about the whole spread of ability.

Ensure that you keep discreet notes about anything you need to be able to remind yourself about students. I use a teacher's app – it has a section where I can write notes about students, and it is totally secure. Before I had this, I used my own codes in the paper planner against names.

"Knowledge is power" – as the man said – the more you have, the better.

Learn names

Look at photos and try and learn at least a few kids' names before they come in. It will make you look prepared and assertive. Don't only learn the names of those who are likely to play you up – that looks like fear! Learn the names of high-flyers, too, or just well-behaved students; there will always be a few names which are distinctive enough to be memorable. Then get the others as soon as possible. Easier said than done if you are new to a school, I know...

But seriously, knowing names, and not just the names of the potentially tricky students, is the most positive thing you can do to make your students feel valued and important. They will appreciate it and reward you for it.

Know your subject

Obviously, you are capable subject specialists; you would not have been appointed to a teaching post were that not the case, nor would you be reading this!

However, it is important to allocate time to researching the resources you will use. Look at the textbooks and associated resources. Read the Schemes of Work. But also look at the files of resources that have been stored over the life of the course by other teachers. Resolve not to be a s lave to one resource. Don't teach to the textbook, or be a "Professor Powerpoint". Quite apart from anything else, you'll bore yourself to death in a while.

It has been proven that students respond better to confident knowledgeable teachers who care enough about them to take the trouble to prepare varied and interesting lessons. They like variety, surprise, anecdotes and humour. A little foray off-piste every now and then will keep students on their toes and will show you how interested they are. (Except for those GCSE and A level students who will put up their hands and say, "Is this going to be in the exam, Sir?" and then put down their pens when you say, "No," and fold their arms until you get back onto the syllabus. And they, frankly, are probably never going to pose behaviour management challenges...)

Seating plans

To make a seating plan or not to make a seating plan? I've been in schools where it was the teacher's choice and also where it was mandatory for every class. When it was up to me I didn't have seating plans, but I am a convert and firmly believe that a seating plan is an essential tool in every teacher's armoury for every class, up to and including year 11.

The paramount reason for this is that your decision to seat students in a certain way is a powerful way of sending an essential message to all students that this is the teacher's space, your space, and you will decide how it is to be used. It's not somewhere they tumble into and sit down with their mates, fully expecting to squeeze in quite a lot of chat between and perhaps during learning tasks, and where the teacher is a slightly irritating necessity cluttering up their space. You are doing everything in your power to ensure students get the maximum learning out of the lesson. You're not a pushover, and you aren't going to seat best friends together just because they tell you they "work really well together. Honest, Miss."

(Actually, I do let them sit together sometimes with a stern warning that if they lapse into chat, I will move them back immediately. Nine times out of ten that happens within ten minutes, and then they don't ask again.)

I look back and reflect uncomfortably that I used to let kids come in and sit wherever they wanted, and that was basically down to my own laziness. It just meant that the entry to and exit from the class became for some simply an extension of the social business that had so engrossed them since they tumbled out of Physics.

When you first meet students all you will have is the barest of information, usually in the form of data. As a first pass at a seating plan, create one that's more or less random (I go boy-girl-boy-girl around the class, starting from the top and working down the register, making sure, obviously, that those with any special needs are accommodated appropriately first). Ensure they sit where you have asked them to, and tell them this is an interim plan, which you will be refining as you get to know them.

Once you are more familiar with the class, create your seating plan carefully to ensure that every student has the best chance of taking as much as they can from your lesson. There are certain rules for this, which you might find helpful:

1. *The first students you should think about should be those with social or learning difficulties. Very often you will have been given some guidance in a protocol document about the students and where it is good for them to sit. Sometimes the nature of the learning or social difficulty will inform where they should be seated. If they are accompanied, even sometimes, by an LSA or TA, then they must be able to get to them easily, or to sit beside them. Consult the LSA or TA.*

2. *After that, you start filling in the other places with those who have behavioural issues, or where two students don't get on, or don't work well together.*

3. *Anybody who is likely to be distracted must be in the direct eye-line of the teacher and there should be no visual obstacle between that student and the teacher. The same applies to attention-seeking students; their attention seeking should not adversely affect the other students between you and them.*

4. *If two students are likely to distract each other, seat them with their backs to one another. It is not nearly as important to have them physically distant from one another. In fact, if they are distant, but in each other's eye-lines, you have the worst possible scenario – two students far away from one another and therefore gesticulating or calling Pacross the room and distracting everyone in between. My particular favourite is directly back to back.*

5. *Either you can go down the top table, middle table, bottom table route; or you can group students according to behaviour; or you can arrange them so that there are two of a similar ability, and*

another two who are slightly above or below. I don't like the first two options. Regardless of whether you call them the Blue Table or the Elephants, Pearls or Knights, they know exactly why they are where they are. Mixing things up is subtler. Some teacher organiser apps give you the option of creating seating plans according to whatever data you have about students by selecting a column of data in your markbook.

6. *At Key Stage Four some teachers choose to have different seating plans for the same class.*

   d. *You can group them according to their* target grade – not *your target, but their own target – this detail is important because a student who is pitching too high or low can find it out themselves when seated with peers, and they can take the necessary action themselves, which is more effective than being told by their teacher. Some colleagues really hate this, but it works for others. Which is rather the point – it should work* for you.

   e. *You can have a lower and a higher achieving student together, which helps both. The lower achieving student can learn from her peer; the higher achieving clarifies their thought processes through explanation. Burst through the door and, dependent on the tasks you have planned, tell them to get into Target Tables or Teaching Tables, or whatever nomenclature you have chosen. Keeps it fresh, and they get variety.*

7. *A horseshoe arrangement works well for professionals in some subject areas. It means the direct focus of the students is the teacher and what they are saying or doing. It also gives the teacher their own stage area, and excellent visibility of all. It does not lend itself well to group work or carousels, but it's never that difficult to move tables and chairs for just one activity or lesson.*

8. *Some teachers find rows with students seated at individual desks, in twos or in fours the optimum arrangement. Like the horseshoe it allows for good visibility and means students can easily focus on the teacher and the work. However, some teachers find it limits their movement around the classroom.*

9. *Never get drawn into a public discussion with a student about seating plans. If a student has a real problem with a specific student, they should approach you privately at the end of the lesson, and you can consider it then.*

10. *Remember: it's your classroom, even if you're only in it for 35 minutes once every two Tuesday mornings. Your classroom, your rules, your decisions.*

❖ Demonstrate consistently the positive behaviour, attitudes and values which are expected of pupils

Be polite.

Be polite to everyone, including the most annoying student in the most annoying class, the one you have come to dread when you see it on your timetable, the class that makes your stomach clench as you see them lining outside the room.

If you have a quick wit and a dry sense of humour, resist the urge to make friends of some in the class at the expense of others. It can be very tempting to tease the loud, hostile but slow-witted child whose party trick is insolence and overt refusal to do anything you ask him to do. It can be very rewarding to meet this behaviour with a light-hearted but deeply felt jibe in response, especially when you notice the other kids getting the joke. However, it will not encourage your problem student, who, seeing the laughter of others, will put more energy into his rudeness, the colourful nature of his epithets and his determination to win at all costs by owning the classroom and making it impossible for you to teach. And when the behaviour escalates and you end up having him removed, spitting and raging, from your classroom, you will know that you are at least in part to blame for the state into which he got himself.

We can only control our own behaviour, and scrupulous politeness and a smile, even if you have to force it, is more likely to de-escalate poor behaviour. If you then seize on something that student gets right in the classroom, you are more likely to get him onside.

Be accountable.

If you haven't managed to mark a set of books yet, be aware and acknowledge that some students will be disappointed that the homework they spent a lot of time making as good as they could get it, is delayed. You're not expected to be superhuman; teachers always try to do more than they are physically able to do and often books don't get marked. Just acknowledge their effort. If you make a mistake when writing something on the board, be grateful when a student points it out. If they hadn't, then the mistake might end up as learning in the students' minds. Consider rewarding eagle-eyed students who point out your mistakes; it encourages students to look more closely and analytically at what you write.

Be a learner.

If a student asks you a question to which you don't know the answer, acknowledge that you don't know it. Give them the chance to see you learning and enjoying it.

Not being omniscient is not a sign that you are somehow failing as a teacher. In fact, you betray a lack of confidence by being unwilling to acknowledge that you don't know something, and by blustering and either guessing or basing your answer on some half-remembered fact, you may mislead a student who is trying to go the extra mile with their work. It is the really confident teachers who are prepared to say, "I don't know the answer to that one. What an excellent question!" You can either ask the student to find out the answer for you so that you can both learn, or for a more complex question you can commit to finding the answer and bringing it back to class.

Be interested.

Exhibit enthusiasm for what you do. Look for the angle that makes even the driest material interesting.

As a languages teacher I can tell you that to utter the word "grammar" in any classroom results in instant yawning. I expect I could say "grammar" to my dog and he would start to yawn and look sleepy. Now, grammar is quite a chunky bit of a language, and it's not really possible to teach languages without a *lot* of grammar lessons. So language teachers have to be creative. Grammar lessons I have heard about or seen have involved clothes pegs, wheels created in class, students lined up against walls, competitions involving headlong dashes to the board... It doesn't really matter – the point is that you're doing something different. You're recognising that this could be dull but rather than just *telling* the students to learn, you're interested enough to do something different.

5

STRICTLY POSITIVE PROGRESS AND OUTCOMES

As Strictly Positive Teachers, we think it's all about the progress of individuals. Ambitious students crave progress and need to be able to see it in order to feel self-worth. The student who is working at a lower level than her peers needs to be able to see that she can make progress on her own terms. So, progress and outcomes need to be transparent to students. If there is a hiccup in a student's progress through the scheme of work, a teacher can acknowledge it and guide the student to make up the deficit and then move forward. If students don't make progress or don't recognise that they're making progress, even when they are, then a sense of failure can easily set in and the self-blame and shame can be toxic. The link between "I am/I was rubbish at school" and "I'm useless" is one which should be avoided at all costs.

Not all students are going to make progress at the same rate, nor should we expect them to, but we should put in place the mechanisms which give all students the chance to make progress on their own terms, and to recognise appropriately the progress that they make as individuals. Teachers who know their students well know what constitutes good progress for an individual and what is only just adequate or below. A Strictly Positive approach demands that we are honest with students and do not praise for praise's sake. If we praise any student for work that is only just adequate, we convey to them the message that we do not expect them to shine. Such praise will have an impact on the students and their mental health, which is completely contrary to what we want to achieve.

❖ Be accountable for pupils' attainment, progress and outcomes

As teachers, our core business is to teach students well enough that they learn from us. Our success as teachers is tied up with our students' success as learners. If they haven't learned, then we have not successfully taught them. Everything else obviously works towards this essential goal: relationship building, classroom management, goal setting – everything.

It makes sense then that we should check regularly that they are learning what we are teaching, and adjust our teaching if it is not meeting this primary objective. Therefore, assessment is an important part of what we do.

> The teaching cycle is:
> - **Planning:** *the teacher plans what they want the students to learn and devises a lesson, or sequence of lessons, to achieve this goal.*
> - **Teaching:** *the teacher teaches the lesson, or sequence of lessons.*
> - **Assessment:** *the teacher assesses the efficacy of the teaching and learning through regular assessment during the lesson or sequence of lessons, and at the end of the lesson or sequence of lessons.*
> - **Reflection:** *after assessment at each point the teacher reflects with the class on any misconceptions or errors and reflects upon how these can be addressed or avoided.*
> - **Planning:** *the teacher uses the results of any assessment that was done in or after the last lesson to plan the next lesson or sequence of lessons.*

The core Strictly Positive method of target setting provides a good baseline for accountability for attainment, progress and outcomes.

> - *In every lesson a student learns something they did not know, or learns to do something they could not do, before that lesson. It doesn't need to be a big thing – it could be an extra, important detail or a different way of doing something. This objective should be completely visible, and students should be able to look at the objective and recognise what learning has taken place.*

- *Each lesson builds on the last and leads to the next. Students should be able to track progress over the course of a series of lessons.*
- *Learning is visible to the student, and they recognise their progress. The flipside of this is that students should recognise when and why.*

Key to the success of this positive approach is ensuring that assessment is effective, and that teacher judgements about what students know are secure. It would be easy to assume that all students are able to do something by the end of the lesson simply because we've taught them, or to rely on either the hands-up responses of a keen minority of the class or a generalised verbal signal from all, where those who are completely lost don't want to admit to it, and so make the same signal as their neighbour.

As professionals responsible for the progress and attainment of *all* the students in each class, we need to be more subtle and exact in our approach. A lot of the conclusions we come to are drawn from experience and a knowledge of the students as well as marking and more formal assessment methods. Teaching is not a science, but an art; expertise deepens as we practise.

Assessment for Learning (AfL), Formative Assessment, Summative Assessment, Diagnostic Assessment, Evaluative Assessment – none of these are the subject of this book, except insofar as they contribute to the core tenets of Strictly Positive Teaching, which are to focus on the positive, to recognise that failure is part of the process and to learn resilience and to work with, rather than against, students' natural ways of being.

There is a temptation to find a few ways of assessing and then stick to them rigidly until you get bored and abandon them to adopt a new raft. This has the benefit of being comfortably predictable for the students so they know what to expect and how your assessment methods work. But the flip side is that these repeated techniques can become tedious not only for the students but also for you.

This is where departments can work together to ensure they have or share good practice and devise a checklist of, say, AfL techniques, which can make their lessons more enjoyable for themselves and for their students, but also can lead them to more effective assessment in the classroom environment. Create a list together. If each teacher in a department of five contributes four or five ideas for assessment, then you will quickly have a varied list of activities which you can deploy in the classroom. Not all activities will suit all teachers of course, and the loud and demonstrative teachers will enjoy activities which quieter and calmer colleagues might find a little challenging. The calming and settling activities that our quieter colleagues employ will be of benefit perhaps to the more theatrical teachers, enabling them to find a quieter space in their professional practice!

Whatever strategies you adopt, the Strictly Positive aspect is that you should be accountable verbally and visibly for the next steps.

❖ Be aware of pupils' capabilities and their prior knowledge, and plan teaching to build on these

We have already discussed the importance of knowing your students from their data before you embark on a course of study. It is important, however, not to extrapolate too much from bare data once you have started, but as you move through a year with a class to use your knowledge of individuals as a guide to what they may be able to do. In other words, it is wise to trust your professional judgement and the evidence of your own eyes over numbers.

Hamish:
On the Special Educational Needs (SEN) register, Hamish had a verbal Cognitive Ability Test score of less than 90. He started year 7 Modern Foreign Language (MFL) with the whole class and when several of his peers were withdrawn to a support group to focus on literacy, he stayed. During this time he excelled in the acquisition of a new language, showing early promise and deriving pleasure from his teacher's approval and praise. His parents were excited to receive emails commending him and his success was self-propagating. Around Christmas his MFL teacher received an email from the Head of English who said that Hamish was going to be withdrawn from MFL in order to join the support set. His MFL teacher demurred, and submitted evidence of his success in MFL. Hamish was left in the MFL group, where his teacher paid particular attention to the grammatical elements of his work and

he continued to thrive. This was a decision taken for positive reasons. He then went on to make better progress in English.

❖ Guide pupils to reflect on the progress they have made and their emerging needs

People like to be able to recognise what they have achieved. It's why people like me write "to do" lists at the beginning of a Saturday, and then add on what they actually did that wasn't on the list somewhere around 3pm, just to reassure themselves that although they didn't do what was (originally) on the list, there are lots of other things that they did do.

Students also like to recognise what they are doing. They like to be told what they are doing and the more this is broken down, the more items they are able to tick off on their academic "to do" list. More importantly, they like to recognise what they *have* done.

Target setting/learning objective works in many ways, and in most schools it changes with irritating frequency according to prevailing taste, fashion and dogma.

There is the "all/most/some will be able to" model, which is beneficial in that it is manifestly differentiated but, in my opinion, problematic in that many of the "all" who don't achieve the "most" objective, let alone the "some" target, somehow end up feeling that although they've learned something in that lesson it's not really good enough. Which might in turn leave them disinclined to reach for something that has been shown to be an unlikely dream.

Many of the PowerPoint lessons I find on teachers' resource sites start with the rather anodyne "LO: to be able to..." or vague reordering of what the teacher intends to teach, rather than a student-friendly objective. Dullsville, Dullsland.

Objective setting is one of those areas where official advice changes with head-spinning rapidity. And don't get me started on learning outcomes versus learning objectives. The Strictly Positive Teacher wants students to know when they come into the room what they are going to learn, and to know that they have learned it when they leave.

After searching for different styles of learning objectives, I need to have a lie-down in a dark room. Here are some examples:

- *The students will recall the four major food groups without error*
- *From a "story-problem" description, students will convert the story to a mathematical manipulation needed to solve the problem*
- *The students will point out the positive and negative points presented in an argument for the abolition of guns*
- *To provide a critical overview of the state of political debate in Britain during the 19th century*
- *Order food and drinks, ask for directions, book accommodation in a hotel and ask for travel details*
- *Increase my overall levels of fitness and vitality healthily and successfully*

Ye Gods.

The first question is: who is the objective for?

- *The student, so they can see their own progress happening in the class?*
- *The teacher, so they can see how well the teaching and learning in that lesson went?*
- *A middle leader, so they can check on the teacher?*
- *A senior leader, so they can check on the department?*
- *Ofsted, so they can check on the school?*

Someone else?

Assuming that the learning objective is set so that *teaching* and *learning* can be visible to the *teacher* and the *learner*, so that the teacher can see that what students have been taught is being learned (you don't really *learn* in a single lesson, do you?) then surely it is very simple to describe what we want to happen in a lesson.

A student should leave the lesson knowing or being able to do something they could not do when they came into the classroom.

My preference is for the objective to open with the statement: "I can...". What follows should be something the students absolutely *cannot* do at the point at which they write down their objective. At the end of the lesson the attention of the class can be directed to the statement, written and kept on the board, so each student can see that they can now do something which they could not do when they walked through the door.

Young people like to recognise that they have learned something, made progress, furthered their understanding to some degree. This is clearly easier to effect in some subjects than others. In languages, for instance, it is easy to quantify that whereas you could count up to 31 in Spanish in the last lesson, by the end of today you can say when your birthday is and how old you are. In Maths, if you have taught a class a method of doing division, then it's unlikely you will be embarking on a separate piece of knowledge so the "I can" statement will focus on how the student can use the prior learning.

So in the MFL classroom, the LZ (*Lernziel*: learning objective) in year 7 in November might be "I can say when my birthday is". At the end of the lesson a child can be asked "Can you?" and they will answer, verbally or in writing: "7th May"; or "on the 7th May"; or "my birthday is on the 7th May"; or "my birthday is on the 7th May. And you? When is yours?" encouraged by their Strictly Positive Teacher to expand their answer to the limit of their ability in that utterance; but everyone "can".

That Maths teacher might have written: "I can solve at least four problems using the new long division method", the Geography teacher: "I can explain what a continental crust is", and so forth. (You can tell I'm on dodgy ground here, can't you? Not my areas of expertise...)

The important thing is that you can challenge a student at the end of the lesson and they can respond to that challenge. They leave your room with a sense of achievement. They have done something important with that 50 minutes. They have a happy memory of your lesson.

In a Strictly Positive Teacher's classroom it is essential that a student achieves, explicitly recognises their own achievements, and expects to achieve the next time they come into the classroom.

This should be explicit. If a Monster Mum (like me) asks their darling on the way home in the car (as I frequently did): "What did you learn in Geography that you didn't know before?" after a brief moment of thought the child should be able to respond. This is made much easier if they have been told, and have written their LO in their books at the beginning of every lesson. LO: I can use a compass. So child brightens up and says, "I can use a compass!"

In other words, the student should be able to characterise the fulfilment of their objective by being able to say, "I can..."

- *I can name the four main food groups*
- *I can order food in a café*
- *I can give ten details about the life of William Shakespeare*
- *I can turn Maths word problems into number problems*

Within a course of study, students should be able to look in their books and see the progression of a course of study. The learning objectives over three weeks in German might look like this:

- *I can name ten sports in German*
- *I can say what sports I play using the first person of the verb "spielen"*
- *I can say what sports I like and don't like using "gern" and "nicht gern"*
- *I can describe how often I do sports, using five time phrases*
- *I can write a short paragraph about my sporting life, using two linking words*
- *I can say what sports other people play using the third person singular of "spielen"*
- *I can write a short paragraph about my friend's sporting life using four linking words*
- *I am ready for a reading assessment on the subject of SPORTS (this is a revision lesson)*

In other words, in every lesson the student has learned something which they didn't know before. They can see how their knowledge builds.

A student should leave the lesson knowing or being able to do something they could not do when they came into the classroom. Then Monster Mum will be happy in the car on the way home, and the student can bask in the knowledge of all that they have learned. Positivity rules!

❖ Demonstrate knowledge and understanding of how pupils learn and how this impacts on teaching

If a Strictly Positive Teacher aims to work with students' natural ways of being, then it is essential that all have some ideas about how children and young people learn.

The problem here is that if you were to pose the apparently simple question "How do children learn?" to educators, educationalists or psychologists, you would receive any number of contradictory answers depending on the point of view, demeanour, age and politics of the respondent. In addition, different theories are constantly being discredited or reintroduced or simply changed. For example, the much-vaunted theory of multiple intelligences was the big thing until a few years ago, when it was debunked, and now anyone who makes reference to it is widely ridiculed as antediluvian and *wrong* on social media. I think this is a shame as most theories contain a nugget of truth, but none of them is ever going to be the last word in education.

Most of what I cite here as fundamental to the science of learning according to current thinking will probably be viewed in a few years as outdated, and a new raft of theories will take its place. The truth is that if we view students as individuals and not a homogeneous mass, and employ a variety of teaching methods, we probably won't go far wrong.

All that a teacher can do is to show that they have thought about the question and tried to include multiple ways of teaching students with different characters, demeanours and ages. We probably all have our ways of doing this. At the beginning of a GCSE course of study, I give my students a questionnaire about the way in which they prefer to learn, and which teaching methods and styles are most effective for them. I prepare a graphical illustration of the results and present them to the class to show that they differ *entirely* in the ways in which they like to learn, and then assure them that I will, at different times, teach using all the methods which they like, but they have to understand that, in order to do this, quite a lot of the time I will be employing methods which they *don't* like, but which others do. At the end of the two years I give them a questionnaire to ask what worked for them. Sometimes their responses match the earlier questionnaire, but often they don't. So I would assert quite strongly that as long as you have used different activities, you are doing the right thing.

Having said that, there are certain activities or ways of working which are generally accepted as important, if with differing emphases.

Learning to learn

Many secondary schools teach learning skills explicitly as an essential part of the initial curriculum and try to ensure as far as possible that students are equipped with the skills which will not only enable them to learn efficiently, but will also help them develop some resilience as learners. In these days of content-rich curricula, this is a wise approach, even if precious time has to be surrendered at the outset.

The four high-level skills that are described as 21st century learning skills are defined as critical thinking, creative thinking, communication and collaboration.

Amongst the skills included in these broad categories are:

- *Critical Thinking*
    - *Analysing: breaking material down to component parts to examine it*
    - *Arguing: choosing a point of view and selecting information to support it*
    - *Classifying: looking for characteristics to enable identification*
    - *Finding patterns and "chunking" information*
    - *Comparing and contrasting*
    - *Defining*
    - *Describing*
    - *Evaluating: coming to conclusions based upon information*
    - *Identifying essential information*
    - *Prioritising: comparing relative importance*
    - *Explaining: conveying methods and conclusions to others*
    - *Problem solving*
    - *Tracking cause and effect*
- *Creative Thinking*
    - *Mind-mapping*
    - *Creating*
    - *Designing*

- o *Entertaining: stories, jokes, singing songs, playing games, role play*
- o *Imagining*
- o *Improvising*
- o *Looking at things from another perspective*
- o *Problem solving*
- o *Questioning*
- *Communicating*
  - o *Choosing the appropriate register when communicating with different individuals or groups*
  - o *Choosing the appropriate medium for communicating a message effectively*
  - o *Evaluating messages: understanding method, purpose and subtext*
  - o *Using appropriate format dependent upon audience and purpose*
  - o *Active listening*
  - o *Reading for meaning*
  - o *Speaking to convey meaning*
  - o *Turn taking: switching from receiving ideas to providing ideas, back and forth between those in the communication situation*
  - o *Using technology: understanding the abilities and limitations of any technological communication, from phone calls to e-mails to instant messages to social media*
  - o *Writing: encoding messages into words, sentences and paragraphs for the purpose of communicating to a person who is removed by distance, time, or both*
  - o *Knowing when it is appropriate to ask for help*
- *Collaborating*
  - o *Allocating resources and responsibilities to ensure all members of a team can work optimally*
  - o *Sharing ideas in a group: rapidly suggesting and writing down ideas without pausing to critique them*
  - o *Decision-making: sorting through the many options provided to the group and arriving at a single option to move forward*

- Delegating: *assigning duties to members of the group and expecting them to fulfil their parts of the task*
- Evaluating *the products, processes and members of the group – coming to a clear sense of what is working well and what improvements could be made*
- Goal setting: *as a group analysing a situation, deciding what outcome is desired and clearly stating an achievable objective*
- Leading a group: *creating an environment in which all members can contribute according to their abilities*
- Managing time: *matching up a list of tasks to a schedule and tracking the progress toward goals*
- Conflict resolution *occurs by using one of the following strategies: asserting, cooperating, compromising, competing, or deferring*
- Team building: *cooperatively working over time to achieve a common goal*

Don't worry about teaching ALL these skills – as I said, something new will come along. I have collected them here to illustrate how these skills can be used to vary the tasks set in a classroom to reinforce learning in a variety of different and engaging ways.

No one is saying that a classroom teacher is accountable for teaching all these skills, but the need for such skills will arise in different lessons and students will, in different environments around the school, acquire many of them. As a Strictly Positive classroom teacher, it is wise to point out to students what skills they are acquiring in the course of doing certain tasks.

"English example – choosing appropriate register – writing a Gothic short story."

"Work skills example – managing time – planning a sales campaign."

"MFL example – classifying – parsing a paragraph to collect common characteristics of word types: pronouns, nouns, verbs, adjectives, etc."

Whatever content you are teaching, find out what your students already know about it

If you are stepping too far ahead of what they know, and there exist gaps in their prior learning which make the acquisition of the new material impossible, then students will fall into those gaps and proper learning can't take place.

If, however, the students are way ahead of you and are already familiar with the content you are introducing, then you will be very excited about how well they are taking in this content (and how well you are teaching it) and will reach some erroneous conclusions about their ability and yours, or they will quickly become bored and lose interest.

In addition, a teacher may find that some pre-existing knowledge is present, but may not discover the fact that that knowledge is incomplete or there are misconceptions. It is important to do this groundwork; if it is not done, you may be trying to build knowledge on shaky foundations.

There are many easy ways of establishing how much your students have already learned, all of which involve asking them!

Say you are starting a unit on Shakespeare in year 7. Students have come from very many primary schools and you don't know how wide the range of knowledge is. Acknowledge this; tell them you need to know how much they've been taught previously. Couch it in those terms – we don't want to make this a "who is cleverest here?" contest. Acknowledge also that there may be students who know very little, if anything, about what is being discussed, and this is not a failure or fault on their part.

- *Give them Post-its® and ask them to write down a fact about the topic you're starting – Shakespeare – and stick it on the board. When everyone who wants to has added their contribution, summarise from the front. You may wish to photograph the board and share it with the class afterwards.*
- *Give them a mini-whiteboard. Ask them in twos to come up with a fact they don't think anyone else will come up with. Ask them to hold up the whiteboards and any duplicates are out. Keep going until you have a winner (or group of winners). If there is great commonality in the answers you can see what is commonly known.*

- *True/False quizzes. Prepare a quiz with True or False answers. These can be done in groups so that individuals are not exposed, but this obviously leads to a less individual assessment of who knows what. Start with easy questions (Shakespeare was born in 1906; Shakespeare lived in Stratford on Avon...) and work towards more difficult ones (Shakespeare wrote tragedies, comedies and histories; Shakespeare wrote Jane Eyre; Macbeth is a Shakespeare play). Everyone who answers incorrectly is out and you work towards a winner (or group of winners).*
- *Written True/False test to be completed in groups and peer-marked.*

❖ Engage students by making the content relevant

It is not controversial to say that our students are bombarded every day by stimuli from their first waking moment to the second before they give in to sleep. The ability to be in contact with your friends constantly has its benefits for those who are good at partitioning their lives, and can make wise decisions about the way they spend their time. Research shows that when social networks and the internet are used to connect with family and friends, young people can benefit from the social support and nurture which this provides. However, things start to go awry when contact with many others, with whom the young person has little real relationship, becomes disproportionately important. FOMO (fear of missing out) can make them slaves to the technological umbilical cord they share with a widening social group, and means this contact between them is the prime mover in their lives.

Add to that the other factors that govern a student's life – relationships with parents and siblings; health or ill-health in the family; trauma; time demanded for other activities from mosque to ice hockey training to orchestra rehearsals to 5am swimming sessions – and you begin to understand that when a student presents himself at the door to your history classroom, the impact on British society of the industrial revolution is probably not uppermost in his mind.

It's not a teacher's responsibility to create balance in a student's home life. Most of our students will probably have parents who will be active in managing this balance between digital communication, family life, work, school and sleep. But not all. One thing is sure. Gone are the days of *Winnie the Pooh* downtime, where "Sometimes I sits and thinks; sometimes I just sits". Many kids don't allow themselves time to be still, time to be bored. Technology has taken care of that, alongside parental expectations.

As Strictly Positive Teachers we recognise that students will not engage with the material we want to teach them just because we decree they should. Students need to perceive some specific relevance which will earn the material a place in their busy brains. So in the chaotic slipstream of a young person's day, we need to make them stop and look at the material we need them to learn.

In order to make students focus on what we are teaching and in order to make good progress and be able to achieve learning in our lessons, we need to engage them by making the learning relevant.

As I've mentioned, perhaps we've all had those older students who put up their hands when you start an anecdote or piece of background information and say, "Is this going to be in the exam?" Those students are operating in a very small sphere of relevance, in that their only motivation to do your subject is to excel in a resulting exam. This is not true of all students, however. Relevance takes many forms:

Relevant to real life

Children learn to speak because they need to communicate with parents. "More!" ..."No!" ... "Need wee wee!"...

They develop a wider vocabulary so they can communicate more precisely and with a wider number of people. "Where is my teddy?"... "My favourite colour is purple"... "I don't like peas"...

 Later they learn the names of specific objects and feelings and abstract ideas because they need to communicate specific needs. "Johnny was mean to me. I'm sad. I need a hug." And so it goes on – the older the child, the more refined their need for communication becomes.

Children learn to add up because they discover that they need to do so for a variety of very practical reasons. If as a toddler you have a row of coloured cars, you learn to count them so you can check they're all there and, if one is missing, so you can accuse your sibling of stealing it. Later you need to know enough to calculate whether you have enough money in coins for the chocolate bar or comic you want to buy.

So far so good – the relevance of some learning is crystal clear and absolutely critical to a person's everyday life. They learn to speak and to interpret speech and they learn to count, add up and take away – because they understand the reasons why this is necessary. In other words, the learning they are taking part in is relevant to their real life.

The challenge in a school is to show young people that what we are teaching them is relevant to their real lives. So, a school that is located near an international business park, for example, may well be able to show that learning modern languages is a good idea and may enhance a student's earning potential.

Mathematics should not be a difficult subject in which to show relevance. Everybody needs to add up to see if they have enough for their groceries or to split a bill in a café. But when they start learning more complex equations, students may well question the relevance to their own lives. A teacher who can illustrate the everyday relevance of their material stands a better chance of engaging their students.

History can be made relevant by mapping concerns of the past onto existing modern-day dilemmas. Today, in 2019, we see a lot of discussion of the parallels between the rise of the alt-right and the development of National Socialism in the 1930s.

The point is that teachers need to look at both these questions from the point of view of the student, and explain to them why it is important – *relevant* – to them to learn French, geography, business studies or art. Why would they do something if they don't understand why they're doing it? It is right that students should ask themselves these questions and it is not enough for us as teachers to tell them they have to learn something because it's on the curriculum. Students have complicated lives and many demands are put upon them, and they are looking for ways to rule things out, and navigate their way through challenging circumstances. Frankly, who can blame them?

Relevant to exam

To a degree, once the child has chosen to study your subject to examination level, arguably it should be less difficult to prove that what you are teaching is relevant. There is a danger, however, of teaching to the exam to the exclusion of all else in your lesson, so the only thing that matters is what's on the curriculum. This is not a way to inculcate a love of your subject. Although it might be a good way of ensuring good examination passes, it may lead to your students deciding that the examination grade is the end of their interest in your subject, and may prevent them taking any further interest in it. That said, it's important that students facing an exam do understand why what you are teaching is important.

So, assuming that you're teaching something you want a student to enjoy and take further as well as wanting them to do well in the exam, there are two, sometimes conflicting, types of relevance to prove. There can barely be a teacher in the country who does not refer to the exam when embarking on teaching some element of their subject. In some subjects this is more explicit than others – English teachers in the UK, for example, will routinely refer to specific questions on specific papers when teaching material, so that students know precisely what is required when they are sitting their exams. This is a good thing in that they can then achieve higher grades than they would otherwise, but arguably a bad thing in that it reduces reading and writing to a mechanical set of rules and does not inculcate a love of language. It is, however, a brave teacher who does not teach in this way. The relevance of good grades in your class is a powerful force for a teacher!

A year 11 boy asked me recently, "Why don't we just learn how to talk to people in French? Why do we spend all the time learning grammar?" He had a particular reason for learning French, in that he knew he was going to move shortly to Canada. He wanted to be able to go about his daily life speaking in French and I had, over the course of a year and a half, failed to show him that what I was teaching him was how to speak French. Instead, he saw that he was being taught how to describe himself and others, how to talk about his hometown and how to comment on the traffic problems in Britain. He struggled to comprehend the need to learn how the perfect and imperfect tense work together, the comparative and superlative of adjectives and how to use intensifiers. He thought what he needed was a set of phrases to meet all social situations. Despite all my explanations and illustrations, he did not see how what I had taught him met his needs – he thought it was irrelevant. No matter what I did, how much homework was repeated or how many sanctions applied, he could not get past what he perceived as a lack of relevance.

This failure to grasp the idea that language requires the knowledge of grammar means that a student is destined to fail if they do not learn the verbs in French. This is fundamental to the language and it is essential that students understand that from the beginning of their studies. He did not succeed because despite all efforts, encouragement and eventually sanctions, he thought he would learn French without this knowledge, and that I was teaching him the wrong thing in the wrong way. He trusted Google Translate, which gave him the answer – how to say a phrase – and he never learned his verbs properly. I'm the teacher; it was my fault.

Relevant to course of study

A course of study doesn't have to lead to an exam, but it probably ends somewhere, and students need to know that what they are doing fits into that journey and why you are teaching them it now, at this moment. They are more likely to engage with the material if they understand why they're being taught it.

This is much easier if you use a textbook in your subject, so that students can see at a glance how the learning builds from where they are at the start to where they need to be by the end of the half-term, term, year. It is sensible if you want your students to grasp the importance of the particular part of the course upon which you are embarking if you explain it explicitly, and in as much detail as is necessary to make them understand why they are doing what they are doing. It takes more thought if you are not using a textbook, and it will require more teacher effort to make this explicit to students. A student-friendly version of the scheme of work, perhaps, can be prepared and given to students and referred to regularly during the year in order to keep them on track.

Relevant to general knowledge

It is an old-fashioned notion that there is a canon of general knowledge to which you can refer and assume that everyone is familiar with what you're saying. It was probably always an old-fashioned idea and always will be – I can remember my father exclaiming in horror at my ignorance when I failed to recognise an excerpt of 19th century poetry, which he deemed essential general knowledge. It's a very similar horror expressed by my kids when I don't know who some well-known reality TV personality is, or when I confess that although I know that *Fortnite* is a computer game, that's all I know about it.

The body of knowledge required of the students of today is enormous. With the whole world of communication technology being an essential part of 21st century general knowledge, the amount we expect our students to know has exploded. Sometimes older people will gasp with derision when they find out that a young person doesn't know the order of the planets from the sun or the sequence of kings and queens of England, but these teenagers or pre-teens can probably operate a range of technological equipment, make and edit a two-minute film and broadcast it, do a bit of light animation programming and help their grandparents to be media literate.

However, it has been shown that students learn well through anecdote or story, and if you can link material to something that many of the students in the room know, then that can be an effective way of rooting an element of your teaching in the brain. If you can link what you're teaching to what they're learning in other subjects, you teach students that knowledge is a continuum, that there are not discrete boundaries. This is a concept that can be transformational in our exam-obsessed, National-Curriculum-focussed educational world. A year 9 project about the Berlin Wall in Germany links neatly to a unit about World War II in history, for instance, and an Art project where students explore creative political graffiti. A year 12 French lesson on "Kiffe Kiffe Demain" about life in 21st century housing developments in Paris can be linked to Geography lessons on urban planning, or History, or Politics lessons about immigration. Links don't have to be explicit or ponderous but simply referred to, to make them interesting, persuasive and relevant.

Many of these interesting deviations from the strict exam path, these little anecdotal asides, may be the one thing that sticks in a student's mind out of all they learned that day.

Learning through play and games

We all like play and games. Everyone wakes up a little when someone suggests a game in the middle of something that may be very important and/or worthy but possibly a bit too serious to keep us on track for 100% of the time. A game in the middle of a lesson is like the comic characters in a serious play – it wakes us up and diverts us, refocussing our attention.

Most subject teachers will have a range of play activities and games they use in their lessons. Parents know a lot about these, because they are the elements children mention when they're talking about their days. They will report what the game was and how it was played. They will show that they enjoyed it. The important thing is that they know how it contributed to the learning – they may or may not be able to explain how, and that may or may not matter. The learning may not be immediately obvious as long as it is real.

In the endless and slightly artificial debate on social media between the "traditionalists" and the "progressives" I have seen this joyless point played out. Traditionalists often decry the use of games because students remember the game and not the learning. To my mind this is not a reason to stop using games and play activities in class, but it does flag up the importance for teachers of making the learning point 100% explicit.

Introduce the activity with a short explanation of what the students are going to do. Then do the activity. Then have a longer discussion with the students of how this contributes to the learning – this should really rely on contributions from the students, rather than your telling them.

In the interest of breaking up lessons to refocus attention, teachers can even choose to include at least one play activity in every lesson, even up to sixth form. As long as it is clear what the learning outcome is, this seems a very sensible way to proceed.

Include varied activities, active involvement

When my own kids developed beyond the point where they could be placed in a certain position and relied upon not to move, I was advised by a very sensible adult to plan stirring and settling activities. The aim was to create a rhythm of activities whereby you were always moving towards either energising them in the interest of pursuing active involvement with parents or others, or calming them so they would be ready to eat or sleep. So you wouldn't put a toddler down for a nap just after breakfast, and you wouldn't be throwing them in the air to delighted gurgles after bath-time and before bed.

So it is with teaching. There is a rhythm to lessons and to the school day. What works with one class on Tuesday in period one at 9.20am may work less well on Friday last period at 2.30pm. If we, as Strictly Positive Teachers are to work with the way students are, then it is wise to recognise the different ways they behave at different times on different days. If you have two year 8 classes, the same lesson plan probably won't work the same in those two different time slots. It is, however, really important to plan a varied diet of activities over the course of a series of lessons. For instance, alternate between passive teaching, listening or reading and active questioning, practice or application, games and play, or assessment.

On a personal note, I think PowerPoint has been a mixed blessing to the art of teaching. While it is a boon in that the teacher can organise the material ahead of time and plan delivery in a methodical way, it can be tempting to rely too heavily on it at the expense of other teaching methods. When I was assuming some leadership responsibility and worrying about the impact it would have on my core business, that of teaching students, I was advised by a senior colleague to plan a half term in advance. I was loath to discuss with her the impossibility of that, except in skeletal outline, and thereby perhaps let slip that she was known across the school as Professor PowerPoint. She was very organised and very well-meaning, and she really cared about her students, but she was absolutely motivated by the need to teach the material, and this need overrode the need to ensure the students were learning. So, yes, it was possible to plan a half term in advance, because there was no real variation in activities, except as directed by the PowerPoint.

PowerPoint is great for introducing material, especially when teachers take the time to include relevant and arresting images and GIFs, and embed other material to make the learning interesting. It is an excellent settling activity, which can be used as a starter and preliminary to other more active learning tasks. Slides should each have a limited number of words – you don't want students reading off a dense paragraph (or, worse, dense paragraphs) from the screen while ignoring everything the teacher is delivering in the more subtle nuanced message. That's the 21st century equivalent of copying from the board. In the same way, when students are set homework or classwork tasks to create a presentation, a limit should be set on the number of words on a screen and there should be explicit dissuasion from copying and pasting material.

Another type of teaching which provokes a great deal of heated, and to my mind pointless, debate is didactic teaching, teaching from the front, chalk and talk – whatever you like to call it. This is the kind of teaching where a teacher stands at the front of a class and for much of a lesson is the deliverer or knowledge and the students are recipients. There was a time a few years back when this type of teaching was regarded as just *Wrong*. It was Wrong for any teacher to talk for more than ten minutes at a stretch. It was said that Ofsted would mark down a teacher who taught in this way. Luckily, wiser counsel seems to have prevailed and the didactic teacher is no longer the educational devil incarnate. Different students respond to different types of teaching in different ways. Some will tell you that this kind of teaching is boring in the extreme, whereas others love being in thrall to a knowledgeable teacher who can enthuse whole classes with the power of their personality and the range of their knowledge.

Many of the most engaging teachers I have observed over the years are didactic teachers. They made me envy their students, made me wish I could go back to the next lesson and continue the fascinating stories they had embarked upon, made me ask myself all sorts of interesting questions.

However, many other engaging teachers whose lessons I've had the privilege to attend have been quite the reverse, setting out ground rules and introducing core concepts before breaking out and involving students in discovering and reinforcing the learning for themselves. In these lessons teachers might aim to include some practical activities, or choose a variety of such activities where possible. Role plays, games, competitions, design activities, quizzes or quiz creation, developing and testing a scenario. It doesn't matter what these activities are, just that they have a specific point, which is directly related to the material being learned and that over time there is a wide variety. A well-judged plenary can take the outcomes of all these activities and turn them into a cohesive and embedded learning experience.

Not all approaches will suit all students. At home I have examples of two very different types of student. My daughter loved a teacher who organised an array of short, timed activities – she loved a carousel and the multi-sensory nature of such a lesson fired all her learning impulses; she found didactic teaching more challenging and would lose focus and start writing notes to her partner. My son's favourite teachers were those who through their character and with their knowledge could hold his attention and engage his imagination – they enabled him to construct a really thorough knowledge of the topic, and he would remember the detail of what he had been taught in the same way as he could recall the plot of a favourite film. He dismissed the carousel type of lesson as gimmicky and didn't feel each activity gave him the time to take things on board.

Flipped lessons

Very in vogue as I write are flipped lessons. In what might be called traditional lessons, a teacher will take responsibility in the class for introducing material for a particular topic. They will teach it and ensure students understand it before sending them home with homework, which builds upon what has been introduced and reinforces it through learning or a series of exercises designed to practise and refine the students' knowledge of that learning point. Perhaps then they will come back into class and there will be a brief assessment, which will show the teacher whether or not the material has been "learned". In other words, students meet the material together with the teacher and then they practise it independently of the teacher in homework. This is generally the way things have been done for a long time. In the past this was partly predicated on the fact that not only was the teacher the owner of the knowledge in that he or she had studied the subject for a long time and was the expert in the room, but also in that the knowledge physically resided in the teacher's head, and was not widely available, as it is now, online.

The challenges of this model are obvious. It relies upon the students being sufficiently receptive to learning to take on the messages the teacher delivers. We have talked about the importance of teacher relationships, peer-to-peer relationships and classroom management on effective teaching; where these basics are not secure, the introduction of key concepts in the classroom are not secure either. It relies also on students having correctly comprehended the material and understood the basic rules that need to be practised. A teacher can try to ensure through AfL that the students have fully understood the lessons, but this is not always foolproof. Moreover, once the students sit down at home to practise the material they may have fundamentally misunderstood some key concept, which can mean that they practise the same error over and over again without any teacher intervention. In other words, they may learn the mistake and not the correct rule and there is no one there to intervene to help them. This mistake, learned through repetition, then has to be unlearned before the correct information can be learned.

In the flipped lesson scenario, students do preparatory work at home for their class. The teacher will set the introductory reading, research, viewing or other activities as a homework with the aim of giving the students the opportunity to understand the material in a quiet place, independently and without the background noise and distraction of a classroom. They then come into the classroom where they will practise or otherwise manipulate the material which they have met and studied at home. So the practice is conducted with the teacher present, ready to correct any misapprehensions and guide the students to address any omissions. This is a great use of the teacher's time and allows them to interact more individually with students to ensure that all get the maximum possible learning out of the teaching/homework process.

It's a great idea. We harness technology to create a 21st century model to replace the out-dated ways of doing things, which were rooted in a long-obsolete model of knowledge and information.

There is one problem. Unfortunately, it's a very old problem, and one that no amount of 21st century technology is likely to address any time soon:

Kids don't always do their homework.

Sometimes they don't do their homework because they're just naughty and they have decided not to do their homework. But occasionally there is a good reason why they have not done their homework – some family or medical emergency or another unavoidable commitment. Perhaps in the traditional model they would have asked for an extension; in the flipped lesson scenario they will be a bit lost.

If in the traditional model the students don't do their homework, what you have is a set of information and principles that haven't been reinforced or practised. If they turn up and it becomes clear they haven't done it, you can give them an extension, or set them the work to do in detention or call them back at lunchtime or after school, and thereby allow them to catch up. If in the flipped model the kids don't do their homework, then you have a lesson plan that assumes certain predefined knowledge and understanding which you are going to test, and which you cannot deliver to some students because they don't have even the most basic knowledge and understanding of the subject. So while the students who have done their homework do exercises that you should be able to spend time examining and correcting, it may be that you have to lay on an introductory session to those who haven't. And because you'll be doing it very quickly so that you can get back to what you were planning to do, they will probably complain that they "don't get it" and from there on in everything proceeds to go horribly wrong.

The Strictly Positive answer to this is to tell those miscreant students that they have a sanction and sympathise with those whose failure to do their homework was not entirely their own fault, and then to hand out printed copies of the executive summary of the material they were supposed to have read/learned/studied, which they can look at independently while you do what you wanted to do with this time. There will still be those cries of "I don't get it!" but students need to understand that to some extent they are responsible for their own learning. This is, however, the only way you can ensure that your lesson will go the way you need it to. It will also mean that for every flipped lesson you will have to create resources that you may not need, which is a pain but not the end of the world. There may be a commandment issued from on high in your school that everyone is going to use the flipped model but, if there isn't, I suggest that you only use it when you have gauged the class and the commitment of the individuals in it to do their homework.

Rote learning

As you may have gathered, I'm a teacher of modern foreign languages. As such I'm passionately pro rote learning. Currently, the biggest problem MFL teachers face is persuading their students that there is no shortcut to learning vocabulary, grammar and structures, that you cannot learn a language by osmosis through being in a room with an MFL teacher or "looking at" vocabulary, grammar and sentence structures. When students ask MFL teachers how come they know French or German or Spanish, they are always dumbstruck at the answer, which is that they probably learned by heart every word they know, starting in school.

Rote learning is not fashionable. It is not widely advocated in secondary schools. It is laborious, it is tedious, it is *hard work*. It is also, I would suggest, something that students need to be able to do.

In the educational twittersphere, which I find a very odd place, there is an ongoing debate about whether or not primary schools should set homework at all. There is a further sub-debate about whether schools should require students to learn spellings and times tables by heart. (Then there is a sub-sub-debate about whether or not anyone is actually suggesting that children should not learn their times tables, but that's Twitter!)

In practice most schools *do* set homework, at least in Key Stage 2, and most of that homework seems to comprise rote learning of spellings and times tables. (There is also a substantial amount of project homework, which seems to result in absurd levels of competitive parenting, as far as I can see, but that's another matter entirely.) The benefits of times tables are obvious. Most people don't really have to think very hard to multiply 9x7, because the answers become automatic. Where some responses are automatic, it frees up more processing power for other, arguably more complex challenges. Where students have become adept at learning spellings, spelling patterns serve the same function, so that students who know that "lily" becomes "lilies" in the plural, and "city" becomes "cities", faced with a word like "indemnity" a student will know the plural is "indemnities" without even giving it a second thought. Where patterns are ingrained through learning and subsequent practice, further material can be easily added and explained by that solid database foundation. Where the initial learning is not secure, adding to it will simply reveal the gaps that need to be filled. In the analogy I always use with my students: if you haven't got your learning foundations in place, then the knowledge house that you build on top will always, sooner or later, collapse.

There is currently a movement counselling the learning of poetry by heart. There is an annual national competition asking students to learn by heart and recite poetry in public. It has been observed in adults with dementia that when they have forgotten even the names of their children and grandchildren, they can recite, in full, poems they learned in their youth. Some advice for people worried about the onset of dementia is to learn a new poem by heart regularly. This is not just another of those "keep your mind active" suggestions, but specific to rote learning.

My mother has Alzheimer's, has long since forgotten the existence of her grandchildren and regularly has to check how I'm related to her when I go to see her. I was recently reduced to tears when during a drive I mentioned how beautiful the daffodils on the grass verges were, and she recited, word for word and with feeling, all four verses of Wordsworth's *Ode to Daffodils*. She learned reams of poetry when she was at school during the war and it's all still there, long after we have all been forgotten.

I'm not suggesting that we add to our students' emotional and mental burden by pointing out ways in which they can retard the onset of dementia, but I believe that these anecdotes serve to illustrate how powerful a learning tool rote learning can be.

Group work

Can open – worms all over the place. One of the questions I ask students who are new to my class is: "Do you find group work useful for learning?" The students seem to understand the term without further prompting, but group work encompasses such a vast array of teaching and learning techniques. The responses are usually 50:50 yes and no to this question. The follow up question "If so, why?" tends often to elicit responses along the lines of "I like working with my friends", which can ring alarm bells.

Unless you are going to restrict yourself to a diet of didactic teaching, exercises and testing, you will probably be setting some kind of group work in your lessons.

The general benefits of group work are easily summarised:
- *Students learn to work together to reach a goal*
- *Students use communication and teamwork skills*
- *Students "teach" one another, and reinforce lessons from the teacher*
- *Students can break down tasks to component parts to tackle more complex problems*
- *Students can deploy their individual talents within a group*

- *Teachers can observe students' skills and weaknesses, which can sharpen teaching*

Any useful group work collaborative activities will therefore be focussed on some of the 21st century skills – the four Cs previously listed (critical thinking, creative thinking, communication and collaboration) and, as I mentioned, the actual activities tend to come and go with fashion. But there are some effects that you need to be alert for:

- Bullying: *much of the peer-to-peer unpleasantness that was brought to my attention as a pastoral leader occurred within group work. A teacher can maintain an overview of the classroom while group work is going on, but it's difficult to be fully aware of all the interactions at each table while you're working with one particular group on what they're doing. One reason why some students really hate group work is that they are often sidelined, their views discounted, and they're subjected to nasty jibes or offhand unpleasantness within their group. For sensitive or quiet students this can be nasty. Add to this the very natural inclination of the teacher to put difficult students with cooperative ones, and there are some students who spend their whole school day offsetting the aggressive or disagreeable behaviour of some others. In pair-work this is not such an issue. But group work can be horrible for them.*
- Exclusion: *it is easy in a group for one or more students to be excluded or not given a role by other students, especially if those students are very ambitious and there is a competitive element to the activity. In any group a leader can emerge and this leader will then decide what is useful (usually what they themselves are doing) and what is not useful or "pointless" (usually what someone else not in their friendship group is doing). They may even take over the activity and not even ask the others for any contribution. Those students who are excluded then switch off completely, dismantle their pen or try to look at their phone or have a conversation with someone in a similar situation in a different group. You as the teacher can easily catch only a glimpse of the outcome of the exclusion and wrongly conclude*

that it is the excluded student who is at fault, being lazy or uncooperative.

- Lethargy: *you've set the task and you move away, giving everyone space before starting to work with individual groups. You get to one group and absolutely nothing has happened, short of a few unrelated chats. You react with some irritation and are told "we didn't get it". You then go into your normal routine about how there is an age-old mechanism for attracting teacher's attention when you need help and "why didn't they...?" and "didn't they know...?" and so forth. They did, obviously, but you constructed that group work task loosely enough for them to agree among themselves that they could get away with not doing it.*

The key to group work is to prepare the tasks very carefully. Explain the task and get students to explain it back to you and provide prompts to those who are likely to say they don't know what they should be doing; in this way failure to do their part of the task is demonstrably down to the student or students. Before starting, assign roles or give a list of roles and make sure groups assign roles between themselves. Name leaders if you are confident that those leaders will be benevolent and won't morph into dictators the moment your back is turned. Make those leaders accountable for the contribution of each member of the group. Think very carefully about how you create your groups. Be aware of vulnerable members of the class and ensure that concern for their well-being is put ahead of any other learning considerations – no teacher wants to be writing statements about a horrendous case of bullying which happened in their lessons, so the extra thought is well worth it.

Practice

Everything requires practice. Today, in a time when a significant number of young people aspire not only to be footballers and film stars, but YouTubers, Instagrammers and social media influencers, this is an inconvenient truth. Malcolm Gladwell, in his book *Outliers*, said that 10,000 hours of practice made someone world-class in any field. Great footballers don't become great footballers by having the odd kickabout at break time. Dancers are made, not born, with the bruised and deformed feet to show for it. Surgeons don't just walk into an operating theatre and wing it. Interpreters become better and faster as they grow in their careers. Nobody can do anything without practice.

So in order to effect academic progress, teachers must provide many and varied opportunities to practise what they have met or learned. What form this practice takes will vary from subject to subject, but the important thing is that practice is built into the teaching cycle.

In music, sport and languages, the element of practice is absolutely obvious – if you are learning an instrument, you need to practise in your own time in order to become more adept at playing. If you practise taking penalties over and over again you should be more likely to score when the chips are down. If you've rehearsed a simple French role-play in a shop, you are more likely to be able to speak and understand when you want to buy a baguette in a boulangerie.

The practice required in some other disciplines is different and may take the form of exam question practice – the ability to understand through practice what a particular maths problem is asking for, or what kind of insight is needed in a particular history essay title.

We cannot, whatever department we are in, presume that our students know how to practise without arming them with the tools to do so effectively.

❖ Incorporating movement in lessons

Puppies have boundless energy, as any dog-owner will tell you. Puppies that are under-exercised will use anything to help them release their pent-up energy. Doors, chair legs, mobile phones, socks, skirting boards, carpets, curtains, ankles – all are objects that can be destroyed in the interest of giving them something active to do. They need to be taken out and exercised regularly or they will vent their frustration in a less positive way. By the time they are older dogs they will be content to sleep for longer and longer times, and the need to move becomes less and less urgent.

In our classes we are still dealing, effectively, with puppies. So we force them to sit still at our peril. Choosing a task that involves controlled movement is a healthy thing for your students and your lesson. I'm not advocating letting students wander around classrooms at their leisure, but in the interest of working with a young person's instincts rather than against them, including the opportunity for movement is helpful and can reinvigorate students within your lesson.

1. *Reporters/Spies: groups work on the same task. They have roles – perhaps scribe, presenter, reporter, researcher. The researcher looks things up in the book/on the internet etc; the scribe makes the work look attractive and clear while the others make contributions. Then the reporters will visit each of the other groups and they choose one idea from somewhere else that their group hasn't thought of. They bring that back to the group and tell the others. The scribe adds that new idea. Then the work is put up on the walls and the presenters remain to explain their thought processes and answer any questions, while the others all look at all the other work. This helps individuals play to their strengths and makes for a nice, buzzy atmosphere.*

2. *Survey: we use this a lot in MFL, as it enables students to practise asking and answering the same question, thereby helping them to learn vocabulary and structures, but it can be used in different contexts, wherever a student can usefully choose from a range of given options. In this way, students can become more aware that there is more than one shade of thought. Inviting students to choose what they believe is the most important factor in a history or geography lesson, or what their opinion is in Personal, Social, Health and Economics (PSHE) or English. This allows students to circulate in a controlled way and gather data. Then they can resume their seats and make bar charts – cross-curricular maths!*

3. *Speed dating: this is useful in practising or rehearsing any knowledge. Opinions, facts or other responses to a question are prepared. Every student has a list of questions and their own responses. They are organised facing another student. They can be named something like "window side" and "door side". They will ask and answer questions for a very short time, just long enough to complete the conversation, then all the window side will move one position and talk to the next person. Next time, the other side gets to move. Some aural reminder is useful to*

signal changeover points – a service bell or horn, for instance, or just clapping.

4. Circles within circles: as speed dating but for smaller classes. The class is arranged in two concentric circles. Students move in different directions until called to stop, and then they talk to the person facing them. A larger class might have two pairs of circles. Can be done to music if you have a relationship with the class that enables you to get away with it!

5. Yes/No walls: ask a closed question and direct students to choose the Yes side or the No side. Add information and see what changes their mind. Or ask students on one side to introduce extra information or persuasion to try and get those on the other side to cross the floor. Excellent for encouraging students to think about justifying their opinions, and building persuasive vocabulary and structures.

6. Arrange yourselves on the spectrum: name two different points of the classroom as extremes of a point of view. Read a statement and ask students to place themselves on the spectrum. When they are arranged, ask them to talk to people either side of them to ensure they are in the right place. They have another chance to move. Then ask individuals to justify why they are where they are, possibly referring to the individuals on either side of them. Excellent for getting students to focus on the smaller details of an issue.

7. Different tables – different questions: linked but different questions are written large on A3 or flip-chart paper. Every student has to go around the room and answer each question on the paper. The papers are stuck to the walls and everyone goes around to read all the shades of opinion, and then return to their places for a whole class discussion of the questions. Excellent for getting students to consider other points of view and therefore develop their own responses.

8. Treasure hunt: clues are arranged on the wall. The answer to each clue takes the student to the next one. Students move around in pairs to compete (or not) to successfully follow the treasure hunt to its conclusion. This takes some preparation but is an engaging activity for students.

The essence of all these exercises is that they should be crisply delivered, with very specific time limits, which shouldn't allow for too much off-task behaviour. A countdown timer on the screen is a useful way of focussing students' minds. And a teacher circulating and listening to discussions, ensuring that everyone is on task and swooping down to praise any really good contributions and note them on the positive side of the board keeps everybody on track.

When in doubt, keep these activities short rather than letting them lose energy. There should always be purpose in the movement. When sending them back to their places, if necessary warn them that you are going to countdown from ten or five or three, and that everybody needs to be back in their place by the time you get to zero.

❖ Encourage pupils to take a responsible and conscientious attitude to their own work and study

It is ironic that successive British governments have, over many years, by increasing the demands made of students and making their teachers more accountable for their grades, have effectively absolved many students of the responsibility for their own learning. By this I mean that teachers now feel as much, if not more, responsibility for their students' grades than the students themselves.

If, in the days before league tables, a student chose not to work hard for his exams, he would underperform or fail them and would probably – grudgingly – admit that the failing was his. Now, if a student chooses not to work hard throughout her education, regardless of her work rate or attitude, her teacher, armed with a Minimum Target Grade, will put all sorts of interventions in place to coax, cajole, threaten and push her through the years of study so that the grade she comes out with at the end of the course of study is as close as possible to that MTG or Predicted Grade, or Projected Grade, or whatever you want to call it. If she doesn't get there, it may well be that the Head Teacher starts asking questions of the teacher, rather than the student, about why she didn't get the grade. The student will tell her parents that the rubbish teaching was the reason for her failure.

This is a profoundly negative state of affairs and means students are disempowered and teachers are overburdened. Obviously, it is important for the teacher to do what they can to help the student achieve their grade, but no one should be in any doubt that it is the student's grade, and not the teacher's. If teachers do too much and exert too much pressure, not only will that student be put under undue pressure, which may affect their mental health, but the grade they get will not be reflective of the work they put in on their own, and at some point in the future it may well be that when that extraordinary level of support is withdrawn, the student realises they absolutely cannot do it on their own. That's a terrible thing to recognise when you're a young adult.

So it is essential that students are trained systematically to take responsibility for their own learning from the earliest possible stage.

We have already looked at some ways of doing this, but let's look again at ways in which educators can encourage students to take a responsible and conscientious attitude to their studies:

- *Linking bits of learning into a cohesive whole, showing explicitly how learning builds*
  - *If a student is to own their studies and their learning, it is important that they have the big picture.*
  - *At the beginning of the year or the course of study, in the cases of GCSE or A Levels and equivalents, go through an overview of what they will be studying and how it will build.*
  - *Then at the beginning of every unit within the year or course of study, look at the elements of the unit which has just finished so the students know what they should have learned or understood, and then show the content of the next unit and how it fits into the whole.*
  - *Use Learning Objectives to show steps within a unit of work so that students can see their knowledge and expertise deepening.*
  - *Draw their attention to what they have already learned as well as what they are about to do. Acknowledge the achievement.*
  - *It's not appropriate to do this every lesson, but now and then it is good to explain how the activities you have planned link*

to build and reinforce learning. I tend to do this when they barrel in on some special day and ask "can we have a fun lesson today, Miss?" just after I've told them that every lesson is fun and that lessons don't plan themselves. Which I assume is what every teacher says in these circumstances.

- *Involve students in their own learning decisions*
  - *You can build enormous trust with a class by discussing at the beginning of a unit or a lesson how to approach it. If you're genuinely deciding which of two or three paths to go down, then asking the students is a good strategy. Following a course on student engagement with Professor Russell Quaglia of the Institute for Student Aspirations, I once gave my year 10 students the contents of the next GCSE module and asked them to decide how we would go about the learning. They took it seriously and came up with an excellent plan. It was incredibly motivating for them and I did the same thing with the same, very disjointed, module of work every following year.*
  - *Sometimes teachers can offer a choice, or a menu even, of activities around the same learning objectives, allowing students to take the path that will suit them best.*
  - *Homework menus are also useful in this way.*
- *Encourage students to set their own targets and hold themselves to account for reaching them*
  - *Rather than setting students specific targets at the beginning of a unit of work, it is interesting to give them a target range, and ask them to set their own target within that range. This gives you interesting information about the students, telling you how ambitious and/or confident they are; if they are the kind of people who work to achieve a target or just set one and then forget about it; how determined they are to meet their own targets; how much it means to them to succeed and how upset they are if they do not meet them.*
  - *Asking a student to set their own target gives them some self-determination and control over their own learning. If they vastly overperform, this can lead to a conversation about setting their sights a bit higher, whereas not meeting*

a target can result in a discussion of how they can do better next time. It would be wise to lead a student to set a lower target for themselves rather than telling them to aim low. That could be disastrous for a student's will to succeed.

- *Assess regularly (not necessarily by testing)*
  - ○ *101 of teaching: keep using different forms of assessment to ensure students are on-track and that there are never any surprises. A student should never be surprised by the result of a formal or summative assessment. They should have identified the points where they needed to take action to get themselves back on track.*
  - ○ *Many courses of study come complete with regular end-of-unit or module assessments. These can be very useful to you and to the students as long as they don't see them as too "high-stakes". It's probably useful to take a little time to help students analyse results and plan next steps, as long as they are real and not a box-ticking exercise. You can tell these by students' "Next Steps" written in their books. "I will work harder next term" is not exactly a useful resolution.*
  - ○ *To mark or not to mark – as I write a debate rages around this subject, and there are teachers who boast proudly that they never mark a book. I like to mark, but as far as possible with comments only so that students actually read the advice in the comments rather than simply looking at the grade and comparing themselves with their friends.*
  - ○ *Peer assessment is a useful strategy here as well, as students can be dragged up by their classmates into a more engaged mindset towards their learning. Make sure peers are working at a similar level, so as not to allow one to crow over and thereby demotivate another.*
- *Be explicit about progress; encourage students to evaluate their own progress against their own targets*
  - ○ *As well as rewarding results, reward progress. Those who underperform in one test and then make good progress in the next should be noticed and applauded, and those whose progress has slowed should also have the benefit of a quiet conversation to check why.*

- Look at, and discuss with students, their progress trajectory over two or more tests. Help them to correct things that are going wrong, or adjust their targets upwards if they are doing really well. Or just celebrate their achievement if that is more appropriate for that sensitive student.

- *Hold students to account for their learning*
  - *Don't let students think you will forget about the classwork or homework they didn't do*
  - *During group work or classroom exercises, if you get to a student who has not done what was asked of her, do not accept any lame excuses of the "I didn't get it", "I'm confused" variety. The student is responsible for their own learning. If they struggled they should have attracted the teacher's attention. A swift sanction – coming back in break or lunchtime or after school to do the exercise – should ensure they know you mean business and prevent them from behaving in the same way in future. Sometimes giving up some time for these catch-up sessions at the beginning of the year means you don't have problems later.*
  - *If he hasn't done his homework, book him into a homework detention. Hopefully your school has realised that detention after school is a far better deterrent from future omissions than lunchtime detention. It may be that there is a department homework detention rota. If there isn't, perhaps you could suggest it. It seems senseless for each colleague to be running their own detentions.*

- *Open questioning and thinking time*
  - *Open questions are great, and the associated silent thinking time will ensure that even the disengaged students take notice and join in.*
  - *If you're asking them a key question, write it on the board so that everyone is crystal clear about what to think about.*

- *Making sure everyone participates*
  - *As previously discussed, have some mechanism for ensuring students know they may be called upon at any time – a random name selector, lolly sticks, any no-hands-up strategy*

- A simple way of emphasising that everybody should be involved is, at the end of the thinking time, to repeat the question before saying the name of the person you are calling upon to answer.
- If you do not get an answer from a student, say you'll go back to them and do!

- Note taking
  - Encouraging students to take notes, from early on, is a powerful way of getting them to take responsibility for their learning. Being able to select what is most important to a learning topic is a valuable skill. Noting key words, dates, vocabulary is something to be encouraged, if not required.
  - Perhaps small notebooks could be given out to facilitate this, or the backs of books used as a place to make notes on lessons.
  - Notes should be looked at to ensure no erroneous information has been noted, but should never be marked. By note-taking a student displays their responsibility for their learning and it disempowers them if the teacher takes ownership of that.

- Talk less; encourage discussion and debate
  - There are so many reasons why it is good to talk less. In this forum what is relevant is that the teacher's instruction and clarification should lead to some kind of manipulation of the teaching material, whether by doing exercises, discussing, practising, collaborating or whatever other means.
  - Encourage students to use prior knowledge to fill in the gaps. Don't be tempted to spoon-feed. That's like when a comedian sets up a punchline in a gag and you chuckle, but then she doesn't trust the audience to get there, and over explains it, and the joke dies.

❖ Teaching for ten years is not the same as teaching the same year ten times

In the days when I used paper planners and before I moved onto my beloved electronic teacher's assistant, I used to keep my planners for several years. I did this because I was, in the main, proud of the lessons I had taught and I thought I could save at least a little time by recycling them with my new classes.

This was a sound idea for someone who was unable to say "no" and therefore quickly became very overburdened. But in practice it never really worked. This was for a number of reasons:

First, the lesson was designed with a specific group of students in mind. Those students would be likely to respond in the way I had planned, and would need the degree of initial direct instruction I had planned, and the reinforcement and practice activities as well. The new classes invariably needed a different balance, and those activities that had gone so well, well... didn't.

Second, I put a great deal of energy into planning lessons, but when I was relying on a previous year's lesson plan I tended not to put that energy in, and then discovered that I hadn't prepared properly and there were crucial points missing.

Also, occasionally I might miss details that had been overtaken by more up-to-date information in the preceding year. These might be adjustments to the course we were doing or the specification of the exams.

Every year there are new ways of doing things, some of which might be suitable for the repeated lesson. But you're missing out on potentially effective learning strategies if you stick slavishly to the way you've always taught.

After a while I took to dumping my paper planners in the recycling in September, and just started all over again in my planning phase. Obviously there were elements of what I had done in previous years that I could reuse, but they were the bare bones upon which I laid the flesh of the current year's requirements.

❖ Keep repeating material until they've got it, or move on and hope they'll catch up as you progress the content?

It is obvious that some students will grasp material much more quickly than others, so the question that faces any Strictly Positive Teacher is: what is in the best interest of students? Is it to keep working at material until everyone has grasped it thoroughly, or move on once it has been introduced, practised and reinforced with assurances that it will be revisited later in the course of study?

According to the Ebbinghaus Forgetting Curve people will forget most of what they learn within 24 hours. Within 20 minutes of learning something we forget 40% of it. After another 40 minutes, we have forgotten half of it. One day later, we will have lost more than 70%. What remains is the 30% which interested us the most, or which chimed with something in us at the time. Theory regarding forgetting time has not moved on a great deal since 1885, and nor have the recommendations as to how to combat it. So it stands to reason that we should expect to teach something at least three times to have any chance of ensuring that our students remember the crucial parts of what we teach. (I'm not pretending that's a mathematical calculation, Mathematicians!)

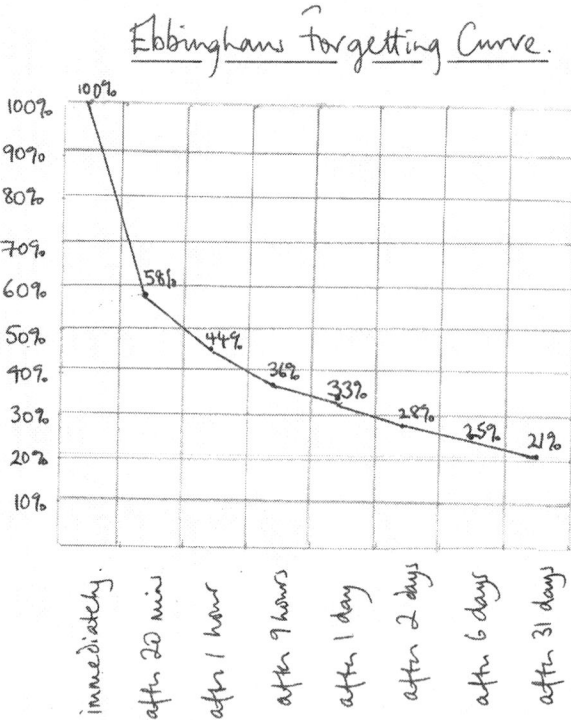

Ebbinghaus forgetting Curve.

Ebbinghaus recommended "overlearning", revisiting material regularly to relearn over and over in order to internalise it. It is what students revising for exams have done for centuries and what intensive learning programmes such as the Japanese Kumon method rely upon.

These days we have access to a wealth of learning systems online, the best of which rely on this theory of little and often resulting in effective learning. There can be scarcely an MFL department in the UK that does not recommend to its students *Memrise* and *Quizlet*, which utilise this and associate it with a competitive element. But *Memrise* and *Quizlet* can be used (and are used) by teachers to devise courses which assist in the retention of keywords in short bursts of effort. These mechanisms can be usefully set for homework. This provides the opportunity for students to learn independently.

❖ Making mistakes should sometimes be celebrated

This is not always true. Clearly we are allowed to be frustrated by the student who listens to your carefully devised instruction, writes out a rule and copies the exemplar sentences or problems, underlining all the relevant words or symbols exactly as suggested or instructed, and then goes on to the exercises designed to reinforce the rule, and completely ignores everything they have just done. That is simply disengaging the brain when the teacher is not directly controlling the activity and not making an effort. They may be the kind of student who regards actual "teaching" as an interruption to their social life, so as soon as a task is set they can turn to their neighbour and say "Anyway..." before continuing their gossip.

However, there are situations in which a student can be congratulated for their error:

1. *The student gives an answer that highlights an error or omission in your teaching. We're not automatons and we make mistakes. It is therefore important to own up to our mistakes and congratulate students when they give an answer which enables us to correct a misapprehension. "Oh, thank you for that, Stacy. That highlights something I forgot to mention. Thank goodness you pointed that out to me!"*

2. *The student tries to extend the learning and applies a rule incorrectly. The jury is out on this. I know many teachers won't go into the extra portion of the material for fear of overloading or confusing the student. Others think you should always supply the missing piece of the jigsaw with a disclaimer that you will go*

into this later in the unit/course. As is so often the case the best advice probably starts with "it depends…". You know your students – some of them will easily be able to assimilate this extra knowledge whereas it will totally confuse others.

3. *The student makes a commonly made mistake. "I'm really glad you said that. It's not quite correct, but it's something so many people do every year. Now, can you look at the rule again and see which bit you got wrong? Thank you so much – it's very helpful to get that answer so early on!"*

6

STRICTLY POSITIVE KNOWLEDGE

There's not really such a thing as Strictly Positive Knowledge, so what we're talking about here is acquiring knowledge and making it available in as student-friendly a way as possible, using proven techniques which will help them in their development through school. Also important is that teachers feel confident and well-equipped – there is nothing more stressful than standing before a class knowing you are only just more knowledgeable than the students in front of you, and that if they ask any questions you might not know the answer.

❖ Pedagogy

Anyone who reads a book like this, which seeks to improve a teacher's practice, is interested in pedagogy so you've got that one cracked.

One thing I find very frustrating about this area is that there are teachers all around the world who seek to improve their practice by buying and reading pedagogical books, but it appears that very few schools have a library section housing a range of pedagogical publications for teachers.

It seems to me self-evident that if they wish to encourage their staff to become ongoing self-improvers, schools should provide the assistance for them to do so. Teacher books are not cheap, which is to be expected as publishers won't be shifting them in the same numbers as the latest Dan Brown blockbuster. Investing in your own improvement as a practitioner therefore takes a chunk out of a teacher's personal budget, especially for younger and more junior colleagues; as this is to help the school, how much more sensible would it be to stock your library with a small selection of such books, suggested by staff, which teachers could access? How encouraging also for students to see that their teachers are interested in improving their practice? So my small whinge to SLTs – think of your teachers when you allocate your library budget and spend a little of it on helping your teachers improve themselves.

When you come to choosing what books you wish to read, I would suggest that you decide what kind of teacher you are. I'm not simply referring to the artificial traditional/progressive divide here, but to your teaching personality. On a course some time ago on student engagement, the group was first asked to decide: "What kind of educator are you?" It was an illuminating question and I found that I immediately had an instinctive answer, as did most of us in the room. It's a good question to ask yourself and see what springs to mind. Over the years I have bought and read a lot of teacher books and there are some which I love and which speak to me, and others which I admire, but which really don't suit the way I am as a practitioner. Everyone will experience the same feelings when approaching the burgeoning canon of supportive professional literature out there. When choosing what recommendations to follow, trust people you think are starting from the same professional character.

For several years my classroom was next door to another teacher who I knew to be an excellent practitioner, with a great deal more experience than me. In the early years I tried to replicate some of the techniques she used with good effect in her lessons. Most of them did not work, and the reason they did not work was that my personality and hers were completely different, so the way we put these techniques into practice had completely different outcomes. I learned after a while to trust my own methods of doing things and to be myself, perhaps tweaking some of her practices to make them fit me and my way of doing things.

Those teachers who are on Twitter or follow blogs will learn what kind of approach appeals to them – I would counsel that you use your reading to decide who you are as an educator. Many of the people whose advice you gravitate to will have published books or will have blogs you find helpful – that's a good place to start choosing what you read to help you progress in your practice. However, an excellent piece of advice I received when starting to use Twitter was to follow people I did *NOT* agree with. Reading opinions with which you do not agree is a very good way of clarifying your own opinions, and sometimes they will surprise, challenge and educate you.

❖ Curriculum Knowledge

Frankly, given the overweening importance to schools of exam results, it is highly unlikely that most teachers will ever be in the situation where they are unsure about the component parts of their subject curricula for SATs, GCSE and A Level. Most teachers will have been on courses to understand the requirements of the subject courses and how to ensure their students make the most progress. There are some organisations schools can sign up to whose explicit goal is to raise exam grades.

It is still a good idea for teachers at the beginning of their careers to ensure they understand how the teaching materials they have at their disposal map onto the requirements of the courses they are teaching. It is also advantageous to the students to keep reminding them how what they are doing fits in with the course, just to keep them on track at all times, and to remind them of the time constraints within which they are working.

In terms of those students who are not engaged on national exam courses, it is worth familiarising yourself with the contents of the National Curriculum as well as the school's Schemes of Work, to ensure you have a broad knowledge of the material you are teaching and why you are teaching it. After all, teachers move schools, and Schemes of Work may vary significantly.

❖ Subject Knowledge

It is not true that more experienced teachers have more subject knowledge than younger teachers. It probably is true that more experienced teachers have a more secure knowledge of the material which they need to teach the year groups they teach. Sometimes the material that is on the curriculum is not what you've been grafting away at in academe but is a slightly random subset of it.

We've already discussed the temptation to teach the same material the same way over many years – teaching the same year ten times as opposed to teaching for ten years. It's easy these days for teachers to keep up-to-date with developments and debates in their subject areas and it is wise to ensure you do so.

Remember, too, that your lesson presentations can easily go out of date – many MFL teachers will pull out their trusty presentation introducing hair and eye colour using the faces of "famous" celebrities only to find that no one in their class of twelve-year-olds knows who that footballer or comedian is any more. What results is a distracting discussion across the room about who anybody is.

There is nothing that says teachers need to stick slavishly to the material in their lesson plan. If something crops up in the lesson that leads you onto an interesting segue about which you have some knowledge, a short diversion is no bad thing. Students like to know that their teachers are knowledgeable, and I dare say most teachers like to show that they have knowledge, too. Win-win all round.

❖ Literacy and Numeracy

Explicit in the teaching standards is the need for all teachers to promote literacy and numeracy in their classes. Hopefully, in most schools there will be teachers in the Maths and English department who are tasked with assisting colleagues in other departments to do so. But whether or not such help exists, it shouldn't be onerous to show that you are active in promoting these areas. If we are not Maths or English teachers, all we need to do is give students little nudges in the right direction.

Literacy

Correct spellings:

Depending on your department policy, correct some or all misspellings in students' work. Perhaps occasionally set homework to learn the spellings of specific keywords or regularly misspelled words. Again, good judgement should be exercised – if you have a student who displays startling insight in a psychology essay, but whose work is riddled with misspellings, some caution should be taken when drawing attention to the misspellings. More attention to the misspellings than to the insights may erroneously convey the impression that that is what is important to you. Strictly Positive Teaching dictates that attention is paid to what a student gets right rather than their mistakes. However, perhaps you could draw attention to specific common words that are misspelled and just suggest that students check spellings.

Sentence structure:

Draw attention to particularly well-constructed sentences, identifying why they are so powerful. Drawing attention to success means students will seek to get more of it, which should be self-perpetuating. However, avoid giving students the impression that long sentences are better than short ones, otherwise what you'll get is a lot of padding: long, long essays with few points and an awful lot of verbiage. (Incidentally, I believe this is increasingly true of literacy teaching where kids are encouraged to demonstrate their expertise with vocabulary by using strings of ambitious adjectives – a mistake, because sometimes, stylistically, less is more.) Many of us will have heard with sinking hearts the student who comes out of her exam and says, in answer to a question as to how they got on, "*I think I did well – I wrote 27 pages and my hand is really sore!*"

Scholarly speech:

Encourage students in discussion to think about how they are going to express themselves before starting a spoken contribution to class debate. Give thinking time and explain to them explicitly that you are asking for more formal speech than the banter they have with their mates. Try in this way to eliminate as many "*like*"s and "*um*"s and "*well, basically, yeah*"s as possible. (Those are my bugbears – everyone has their own. I've even had students start essays with, "*Well, basically…*")

Specific vocabulary:

Congratulate the student who refers to "enormous" or "rapid" progress instead of "lots of" progress. A double tick, or your equivalent, whenever a student includes more specific terminology.

Numeracy

Adding, taking away and dividing: all that teachers of other subjects need to do when the opportunity for this crops up is to refer explicitly to the fact that they are doing something mathematical.

Graphs:

There will be times in most subjects where it is possible to manipulate data and include graphical representation of something, whether it be the results of a customer survey in year 10 Business Studies, or what pets year 7 French have. Encouraging students to create graphs and specifically referring to this as a skill of numeracy is always helpful.

Statistics:

There will often be opportunities to use statistics in a lesson. Again, a simple reminder that this is maths helps convey the message that maths and numeracy are important in life, not just in maths lessons.

7

STRICTLY POSITIVE LESSON PLANNING AND TEACHING

Lesson planning is more than looking at where you got to last time and then estimating how long the next activities in the textbook will take you. It's more than using the same few techniques over and over again to cover the material.

The Strictly Positive Teacher takes time and uses teaching and assessment to plan lessons. "Failing to plan is planning to fail" was one of the aphorisms we lived by when I worked for a large corporation back in the day. It's trite but, like so many such sayings, contains more than a grain of truth. It could be argued that planning is the most important part of what teachers do, and it is something that too many of us skimp on.

❖ Impart knowledge and develop understanding through effective use of lesson time

When you embark on your career as a PGCE student or an NQT, lesson planning is a very laborious and time-consuming task that takes up an inordinate amount of time. There can hardly be a qualified teacher in our schools who has not, as a student, been up at 11pm laminating, cutting out, photocopying or colouring resources for their next lesson. My Head of Department still prepares a lesson plan for every lesson she teaches, which ensures that her lessons are always crisp, purposeful and well planned, with all resources carefully prepared. I am full of admiration that she does that while running a department!

Too many experienced practitioners think they no longer need to plan their lessons as carefully as they used to. They're probably right that they won't grind to a halt in the middle of a lesson, looking at the class with no idea what to do next, but equally they are probably not giving their students the best service as professionals. In addition, there are professionals who have taken on extra responsibilities which mean they have to be reactive to situations which may arise during the school day. For them, lesson planning feels like a luxury. There are many of us who have found ourselves running into a class at the last minute after dealing with something that has arisen out of our additional responsibility, and looking at the class with a panicked smile:

"So... where did we get to last time? Can someone recap?"

And then you take up the lesson on the next page in the textbook. I'm not proud of it, and it didn't happen many times, but it did happen. It wasn't awful; nobody died, but it's stressful and you realise that perhaps you're not the teacher you thought you were.

Another pitfall to planning in a rush, or failing to plan, is that you can easily find yourself in the situation where you come to rely on a tiny array of techniques that you stick into every lesson plan you create. If you find yourself getting bored by your own lessons, it's time to change. Then you will come across another technique and that will be used in every lesson. The answer is, as a department, to spend subject time coming up with a long list of ideas divided into separate areas: introducing material, practising material, games and play etc. Copy it and stick it to your desk, and you have a pick 'n' mix of ideas. You can add to this periodically with ideas from other departments, from friends, social media, conferences – anywhere you go. If you search online textbook/teaching websites sometimes you'll find some gems of ideas hidden among the small print.

Keeping things varied is a way of sustaining not only the students' interest in what you're teaching, but also your own. It makes planning, if not quicker, then definitely more satisfying for yourself.

I would suggest there are some key planning milestones which every lesson should include:

- *A goal, which is your starting point. What are the students going to learn in this lesson that is new? Start there*
- *How will I get them there? Plan backwards and choose activities that will get them there*

- *How will I know they've got there? The assessment part of the lesson*
- *How will I start the next lesson by linking what has gone before to the new learning? The link between last lesson and this one – your starter.*

Once you know the answers to these questions, which won't take you long, then you structure your lesson, which might look something like this:

1. *Starter: refer to last lesson and recap*
2. *Link to current lesson*
3. *State or elicit the goal of today's lesson*
4. *Introduce material*
5. *Practise material/Fun activity*
6. *AfL or mini-assessment*
7. *Plenary: recap*

Some of these points will only be a line or so, and some will take a larger chunk of your lesson, but however you structure it, structure it, so that you know fairly clearly how things are going to go.

I like to include a fun activity in every lesson. Yes, really. I can almost hear the jeers of a large chunk of the profession as I write that. It doesn't mean I have a full-on game in every lesson but something, usually manipulating or interacting with the knowledge or skills vital to that lesson, which will energise students, wake them up and involve those who are habitually less involved. Remember, being Strictly Positive means working with kids the way they are, not requiring them to be as you need them to be – drawing them in, not pushing them.

Fun elements may include quizzes, competitions, games, active tasks. My students say they like "playing with the ball", which is when I throw a ball to them as I ask a question and they throw it back as they answer it. I call it questioning; they call it play.

It has been shown that students retain information they've learned in play. They also learn from anecdote or analogy. Have a store of those at hand. It's unlikely you'll be able to use one in every lesson but every now and then you can pull one out of the bag. A history teacher I know, one of the most superb teachers I've ever met, recounts history using the present tense as a story. (I think most history teachers do this, don't they?) His lessons are among the most engaging and involving it has been my privilege to experience. His students get fantastic grades because they are constantly interested in and engaged with the stories he has to tell. (A little aside here: why does English have separate words for "story" and "history" when in many languages they are one and the same?)

❖ Promote a love of learning and children's intellectual curiosity

Presumably, most of us want our students to love the subject we teach. It would be a sad old existence if we were not interested in engaging them and inspiring them. One of the happiest moments of my teaching career was sitting in a year 8 Parents' Evening with a young man and his mother and hearing him tell me that he wanted to do German for A Level. He was absolutely certain of this future. Not only did he fulfil this ambition, but he went on to university and was named the top linguist of his cohort in his first year. He has learned several other languages and is now a far, far better linguist than me. That is what we want to achieve!

We probably don't get many of those, but we can do what we can to engage and inspire to a greater or lesser degree all the students in our classes. In addition to inspiring our students with a love of our own subjects we can also do what we can to promote a love of learning in general, to pique their curiosity, to ask the interesting questions which will make them look at the world around them in a more wondering way.

One of the ways we can do this is by briefly segueing from the matter in hand and recounting stories and anecdotes, using interesting analogies or presenting surprising words or facts.

Any student who has ever been taught by me will probably be able to tell you that the old German word for hovercraft (before they started using the infinitely more boring "*das Hovercraft*") is "*das Luftkissenfahrzeug*". This is because when I introduce the idea of compound words in German and the fact that you make a German word very literally by assembling component parts, I ask them what they think a *Luft Kissen Fahr Zeug* – Air Cushion Travel Thing – might be. After a lively discussion I reveal that it is a hovercraft and we all have a good laugh. But after that, faced with a long German compound word, the students know to try and break it down into its component parts to work out meaning.

We all have our little stories to tell and our little factual oddities and they will often be what remain after a lot of what we teach has gone. "Memory is the residue of thought," said Daniel T. Willingham in his excellent book *Why Don't Students Like School?* He maintains that one of the reasons students don't like school is that learning is hard work, and therefore not attractive to young people. We would do well to try and consider what dictates what gets caught in our memories, and how, and how we can use this knowledge.

So we need to teach in as engaging a way as we can, in order to encourage students to retain as much as possible of what we want them to know. This goes for all students in all classes. But what about those students who exhibit the flicker of something else, a passion for the subject, a fascination, an aptitude which is difficult to address in the hubbub of a mixed-ability classroom?

Most departments will have Gifted and Talented policies, which will decree what teachers should do when they have someone who displays additional ability in their subject and there will be a programme of activities or resources which will be appropriate. However, as teachers – or, even better, as departments – it would be wise to devise as you go along a list of resources or links to other material for each topic area which the most interested students could access. I would counsel that teachers shouldn't make these tasks something that will be assessed or checked, but to adopt a more encouraging, non-judgmental approach to the business of acquiring extra knowledge. Maybe ask the student to stay for a moment and ask if they've had a chance to look at the material, if they'd like a chance to discuss it, or if they'd like to do something related to this material for other students. Some will and some won't. But an authoritarian, evaluative approach to the business of acquiring a more profound knowledge or acquaintance with the subject may well be counterproductive and lead to an impression that ability is a burden. Tread lightly. If your gifted students are painfully shy, put your links and resources on your Virtual Learning Area and simply direct them there with the assurance that if they want to discuss anything with you, they can.

It may appear that having a gifted and talented student requires you to do a great deal more work, but I would argue that the emotional and mental benefits to a teacher of instilling a real love of learning in a student more than outweigh the extra workload.

❖ Set homework and plan other out-of-class activities to consolidate and extend the knowledge and understanding pupils have acquired

We all have our private feelings about homework. It's probably the element of teaching which is the most onerous, involves the teacher in more work, and necessitates more follow-up than any other aspect of teaching. Homework needs to be set for all. It needs to be collected from all, and then arrangements made for extensions or sanctions for those who have not done it. It needs to be assessed and feedback needs to be given. A massive burden for all, and especially egregious for those of us who have read John Hattie's *Visible Learning For Teachers* and noted that research suggests that the effect on grades of homework is at best small; at worst negligible. In Finland, one of the educational superpowers of the world visited by Lucy Crehan and discussed in her book *Cleverlands*, there is no homework. Instead, students are advised to go home, play football or anything else, read a book, climb a tree, be with their parents, talk, learn to be part of society.

However, we live in Britain and here I'm quoting one element of the Ofsted criteria which dictates that at the end of a school day, students should go home or to their library and continue the day's learning, to "consolidate and extend" what they have done in school. Students know they're expected to do homework and most have been doing it since they were in primary school. Some of them accept it, welcome it even, and they probably have parental support at home, as well as a schedule, a routine and a quiet place to do it. Some will have, at best, the active participation of a parent or carer in the execution of that homework. In this situation homework can represent a productive way for parents to involve themselves in the academic lives of their children and can indeed be a bonding experience for the family. Many students, however, have none of those things and need to shoehorn their homework into a chaotic and busy homelife, trying to reclaim time from the family demands, to find a calm place to focus on a history essay plan or get time on the family computer to do their *MyMaths* problems. Some simply have no interest in doing homework at all when they get out of the school gates and have no adult interest at home in whether they do it or not, and they accept the resulting sanctions as a part of their school days, along with many of their mates.

The problem then with homework as far as I see it from a Strictly Positive perspective is that you have no realistic control over whether or not students do it; that is almost entirely down to their domestic situation. You have an immediate division in your classroom between those who make faster progress because of no virtue of their own but because they have support at home, and those who don't. And those who *do* do their homework are better equipped for the next lessons, and those who don't aren't; we thereby set in motion two separate paths: the fast track and the slow lane, and it has little if anything to do with ability or motivation. It has little to do with school at all even, but all to do with family attitude, education or means.

So for a Strictly Positive Teacher the question is: how do you minimise the negative impact of setting homework on some students? And the answer has to be in the nature and quality of the tasks.

Learning

You may gather that I'm generally not a fan of homework, with one significant exception in MFL – learning by heart. If I introduce ten words in a year 7 lesson, homework will be to learn ten words and then there will be a vocab test at the start of the next lesson. This is an area in which students can harness technology to make homework work for them. In any MFL lesson students will meet new vocabulary, grammar and structures and it is in the nature of the subject that success requires that they internalise this material. There is no quick way of doing this except rote learning. Luckily for us, the internet provides many websites – some of them available as apps – that will help students to do just this, so they can learn on the bus, in the car or sitting around at lunchtime. In addition, they can turn learning vocabulary into a competitive sport. So just about any homework I set will be learning and points will be awarded for progress.

There are many cross-subject websites that enable students to learn material. These provide the mechanism for teachers to construct with relative ease study sets for their students, which they can access in a number of ways. *Quizlet* introduces material in an automated flashcard mode, tests spelling and matching and then provides games which students use to refine their mastery. It's a model that works exceptionally well. *Memrise* started out as being for MFL but has expanded as other disciplines recognised that they could use it to their advantage. YouTube is also excellent for learning, with a host of clear and engaging videos on all manner of subjects. Students especially enjoy videos by their own teachers! These are only a few options.

Flipped Learning

Flipped learning means that students do preparatory work at home for their class, and thereby do some of the research they need independently. The idea is, as discussed earlier in Chapter 5, that this can be done in a quiet focussed situation, and the hard work – manipulating and practising the material – can then be done in a supported situation with the teacher available to correct any misapprehensions or address omissions. This is particularly advocated when working with students further up the school, in preparation for GCSE and A Level. In principle it works very well, but it is predicated on the fact that students are motivated and engaged enough to work with the material in order to understand it. In practice I have had lessons derailed when one student says to me as she comes in the door:

"I didn't get the homework, Miss."

Another student, "Same!"

Me: "What did you not get?"

Student: "Any of it."

And then I have three choices: press ahead and give the two who haven't done the preparation time to catch up but no time to practise; assign those who have done the work to explain it to those who haven't; or spend valuable time recapping and going over what should have been done at home.

With regard to flipped learning, my advice would be, as ever, to proceed based upon your knowledge of your own students. If you are confident they will all do the work, flip away; if not, think twice.

Research

In these days of easy access to the internet, research becomes an easy task to set. Research can be individualised so that each student, or group of students, researches a different element of what you are teaching. Or you can set a research task to a group and they will divide the burden between themselves. The downside of the group task is obviously that if one or two members of the group do not do the research necessary for some follow-up classroom activity, then they will be very unpopular with the rest of their group.

Another consideration of setting research as a task is what you want students to do with the results of their research. Try to guard against the tendency of some to find some material that approximates to what they should be learning and then cutting and pasting vast, unfocussed, irrelevant tranches of text into their presentation or essay. It's probably worth spending some time with a class and giving them criteria for their research methods so they get the most out of the process.

Homework Menu

To get around some of the challenges of setting homework you may elect to set a homework menu. This allows students a choice in the way in which they manipulate the learning material.

A homework menu does not have to be a complex thing. It may contain a task with not much writing, a creative design task, a writing task and perhaps a performance task.

So, for example, back in year 7 English, after a lesson on Shakespeare's Globe, the homework menu might look like this:

Choose from one of the following tasks:
- *List the parts of the theatre in your books, along with a short explanation of the function of each*
- *In your exercise book, draw, colour and label a plan of the Globe theatre using the keywords for different areas*
- *You have just come back from a visit to the Globe to see Mr Shakespeare's latest play in the 16th century. Describe the experience in a maximum of two pages of your exercise book*

- *Record a short audio tour of the Globe for a modern-day audience, focussing on how the theatre was used in Shakespeare's day. Keep it to a maximum of two minutes. Email the recording to me*

Homework No-nos

Tasks that should never ever EVER be set as homework:
- *Anything that relies on students or parents buying anything*
- *Anything that relies on assistance to construct*
- *Anything that is so open-ended conscientious students will spend hours on it, while some will do almost nothing*
- *Anything that does not pertain either to what you have just done or what you are about to do*

Add to that tasks which should be avoided out of kindness to teachers:
- *Open-ended tasks that require lots of marking*
- *Complex tasks that require a lot of explanation and will probably go wrong anyway*
- *Anything that involves you in extra work*

❖ Reflect systematically on the effectiveness of lessons and approaches to teaching

We have all come out of a lesson and thrown the staffroom door open to declare that we have just had a terrible lesson and rant about the behaviour of Isaac in year 9 and received lots of sympathy and empathy from our beleaguered colleagues who have had similar experiences. We are good at metaphorically holding the hands of those of our colleagues who are having a rough day, week, term.

It is probably less likely that we stroll into that staffroom, head high, broad smile on our faces and declare that we've just had a fantastic lesson, and Isaac in year 9 just did the most amazing thing. It's somehow un-teacherly to trumpet success; somehow it seems as if you're showing off, and that's not something we teachers do.

The irony is that when we have these moans about a class that went badly, the inference which is drawn is that the teacher is saying that it's not the teacher's fault, that there were other factors, usually one or a few students, which led to the downfall of the lesson. When, however, we have a really good lesson, we're shy to say so, because we think we're saying to our colleagues, "I had a great lesson because I'm a great teacher."

The truth, as is nearly always the case, probably lies in the middle. I think we should be less shy of saying when a lesson went really well. We could usefully have fewer conversations about Isaac or John or Stacy or Takisha, and more about what made a lesson go well.

When I mentor teachers new to our profession, and at the end of a lesson I ask them to reflect upon the lesson, their immediate instinct is to tell me what went awry, and they think very carefully about what *didn't* go as planned and are able to pinpoint the moment it went wrong and the reason, and with some guidance they can tell me how to avoid such an eventuality in the future. And all that is very, very important.

However, the flip side is that it is equally important to reflect on all the things that went *right* and to analyse in just as forensic a way all the reasons why an activity or an interaction with a pupil went well. For some reason new teachers, and their older colleagues as well, are loath to think about all the ways they are getting things right and to work out how to replicate these elements in order to continue this success.

This is not just mindless optimistic positivity. If things go right and you dismiss your success as incidental while focussing rigorously on the negatives in the same lesson and resolving to find ways of correcting your practice in certain areas, you are only studying half the evidence of your lesson, and what you learn for your professional practice from that lesson will only be half as effective.

Mentors should lead on this. Notes about what went well and thoughts as to what would be even better are good, but both halves of the equation yield evidence, and new teachers are usefully guided to reflect on *why things went right*, as well as why things went wrong.

The more experienced teacher who reads teaching manuals should also spend more time reflecting on what went well in their lessons. It would improve morale if everyone were required to do so, rather than being urged into constant joyless analysis of how to address perceived failings.

If I were in charge, every subject meeting agenda in the land would have a standing item, next to Health and Safety, where every teacher, trainee and heads of department included, would pick one lesson which went well, and describe why.

❖ Contribute to the design and provision of an engaging curriculum within the relevant subject area(s)

Strictly Positive Teaching is not only intended to improve the lives of the students in our schools, and to work with the ways in which their natural psychology and physical needs demand; it should also make teachers' lives easier and more enjoyable.

One of the elements which can contribute significantly to the well-being of professionals in their workplace is the feeling of being part of a collaborative endeavour. The sense of a shared mission, one rooted in professional expertise and vigour, is a powerful driver for self-improvement and refocussing on the goal of improving students' learning and their consequent life chances. In addition, in purely practical terms, the fact that teachers have limited time allocated to planning and curriculum design works against both the devising of an engaging curriculum and teacher well-being. Instead, too much training time is often directed to Continuing Professional Development (CPD) or the implementation of top-down directed initiatives. This means that many teachers spend their own time in evenings and early mornings planning lessons and creating resources, at the same time as their colleagues. With a bit of foresight and a reasonable amount of time for joint planning, schemes of work and resources could be more precisely discussed and planned, with time allocated for each to contribute. Without the requisite time being provided this simply cannot happen.

What happens then in schools is that the demands for endless paperwork and justification of their own professional practice leads teachers to close their classroom doors against all comers for fear that they will be judged. It is therefore up to enlightened leaders to ensure that good ideas, creativity, innovation and the sharing of good practice are valued in their schools, and such value must be manifest in *time* provided for such a purpose.

This is essential. If already overloaded teachers are told they must somehow find a way to squeeze this into their already packed schedule, then it becomes another burden which will either not be done or be done grudgingly and cynically. The opportunity to share and experiment should be provided in such a way as to be welcomed by teachers, to excite them and enthuse them.

Leaders can show their commitment to the sharing of good practice by dedicating time:

- *Time is set aside for teachers to meet regularly to engage in joint lesson planning and joint lesson observation and joint reflection*
- *Cover should be provided for this joint observation*
- *Teachers' time for these activities is protected, and other aspects of their workload are managed to ensure that professionals are able to prioritise their pedagogical improvement*

Other important considerations relate to who benefits from this process. Whereas in the past there has historically been a mentor-apprentice idea of the sharing of good practice, where an older teacher takes a teacher new to the profession and passes on their expertise, this is no longer necessarily the case. (I say not "necessarily" the case, because some schools unwisely discard or undervalue the knowledge and expertise of their older colleagues in a headlong race for novelty and over-eager embracing of educational initiatives, some of which may be truly valuable while others prove to be fads. Those longer-standing teachers whose teaching may look "overly didactic" or conventional are often the most successful and engaging professionals in a school, and for the sake of our students we should offer them the most varied pedagogical diet.) However, in the rapidly changing world which we and our young people inhabit, and which we must acknowledge, we need to adapt our teaching methods. Some schools are so blinded by technology and novelty that they feel the majority of skills transfer will go the other way, and those fresh and shiny ideas brought in by NQTs fresh from their initial teacher training will make those who've been grafting at the chalk-face (not that such a thing even exists any more... whiteboard-face doesn't have the same ring to it) change their practice altogether.

There should be a clear understanding that this is a democratic process where everyone can learn from everyone else and nobody is the master. All should expect surprises and all should expect to give to and take from the process.

So how might this sharing of pedagogical enthusiasm look? There are various models for this kind of sharing.

Teaching and Learning Groups

T&L groups represent the bare minimum. Representatives of each department get together to share expertise. As so often is the case with groups of people nominated for a particular responsibility, these are duty gigs and meetings are often attended without enthusiasm by people who say as little as possible, hoping the meeting will come to a swift conclusion. Also too often hijacked by T&L leaders who will engineer them to achieve tick-box agreement with something they want to do as a vanity project.

Teachmeets

With a tight focus, teachmeets can be very successful. Contributors will prepare short presentations (one to two minutes) on a specific issue – "Raising independence among year 12 students"; "improving writing outcomes in KS3" – and attendees will have a large range of ideas to try out by the end of an hour. There's no quality control though, and no follow up or reflection to assess its efficacy.

Department Groups

Within departments or faculties, teachers do joint preparation of a lesson which they all teach and whose efficacy they evaluate as a group. Sometimes they can co-teach the same lesson to two different groups, or they can teach each other's groups. Great for team spirit. Not great when you're the leader and only member of the DT department.

Lesson Study

The lesson study model, originating in Japan from use of Confucian ideas, has become more popular over the last ten years. Three teachers from different departments will together choose a particular class and will identify an educational or behavioural need within that class. They will research and choose a particular pedagogical approach which they believe will address that need. They will agree on a way in which they will evaluate the success of their approach. They identify case study students and familiarise themselves with baseline data pertaining to those individuals. Together they will plan lessons for each teacher which will use the new approach. Each will teach their lesson while observed by the other two. They will then reflect on the success of the approach using data and interviews with the case study pupils, refine the approach and restart the cycle. This is a highly academic cooperation and can yield significant benefits for all involved. Success requires that all put ego aside and remain open to approaches that may be far outside their normal sphere of operation. Which is rather the point. Personality is important when putting teachers together; if colleagues don't like one another, this is doomed to failure.

Teaching Triads

I learned about teaching triads some years ago when I attended the Outstanding Teacher Programme devised by Peter Blenkinsop of ManYana Education. Triads resemble the lesson study groups in several ways. They are groups of three teachers from different departments and they plan, teach, observe and reflect together. But whereas the focus of the lesson study is a particular class, the focus of teaching triads is much more the individual teachers and their own pedagogy. It is a supportive, non-judgemental mechanism that enables teachers to take risks with their own practice. In their initial meeting each teacher will identify something in their own teaching with which they are unhappy or which they shy away from. This might be group work or movement in the classroom or using the interactive whiteboard, or it might be an element of behaviour management. This is an opportunity for a teacher to acknowledge, rather than hide, a weakness and seek to address it. The teacher then plans a lesson or portion of a lesson with the other colleagues which addresses this aspect of their practice and teaches it or co-teaches it (or even asks a colleague to teach it), and the group reconvenes to discuss and reflect. This is an approach built on trust rather than a requirement for compliance and, in order to be successful, needs to be free from the heavy hand of senior leadership demands for accountability.

If school leaders are prepared to make the investment in time needed for such approaches as lesson study and teaching triads, they can see substantial benefits. Students see an invigorated staff, bursting with enthusiasm and new ideas; they are surprised and inspired. Teachers enjoy the chance to feel like teaching professionals whose experience as well as their innovation is valued and nurtured. They enjoy discussing pedagogy.

If leaders try to cut corners or squeeze such initiatives of the requisite time, they will not succeed and might as well not start. If there is a culture within a school where a senior leader in charge of teaching and learning presumes that teachers need to acquire specific knowledge in a one-off, tightly focussed, rigorously assessed framework, then this peer-to-peer, enquiring, experimental environment will not survive.

8

STRICTLY POSITIVE DIFFERENTIATION

Every child matters. When a phrase becomes a slogan or a policy, sometimes the words lose their meaning. And this is a tragedy, because the idea that every child matters is at the heart of Strictly Positive Teaching – indeed, it should be at the heart of the business of teaching itself. By taking positive control of our classrooms we can all adapt the ways in which we teach to ensure the students in our care – because if they are in our classroom then they are in our care – are able to access the material we are making available to them.

Differentiation can be infinite, and the way in which schools are set up in 2019 does not allow teachers and support staff enough preparation time for each lesson to allow them to differentiate as fully as would be desirable. So we have to start off by looking at groups, ensuring we put in place mechanisms to help those groups learn effectively. After that, perhaps, we can go further if we have time and resources.

As a teacher's knowledge of his or her students deepens it may become easier to refine differentiation in certain reactive ways, basing interventions on individual relationships. This is not always possible.

What is always important, however, is that you do your homework and you try.

❖ Know when and how to differentiate appropriately, using approaches which enable pupils to be taught effectively

There cannot be many schools left in the UK which do not provide their teacher with sophisticated data to guide them as to what an individual's particular needs are.

Among the data available will be:

- *Prior attainment, probably in the form of end-of-key-stage results. Many English, Maths and Science teachers believe it is misguided to attribute too much importance to Key Stage 2 SATs' results, as so much effort is put into bringing students in Year 6 to peak performance in SATs, that sometimes these results are not secure as an indicator of future attainment.*

- *CAT scores: verbal (useful for English, Languages, Humanities, Drama); non-verbal (raw problem solving "processing power" – the most abstract measurement, and arguably the most important); quantitative (useful for Maths and Sciences). There will be an average CAT score, but it is worth the seconds it takes to check if there are disparities within that average. Large disparities can create their own problems for a child.*

- *Gifted and talented: students whose previous teachers and schools have identified them as high achievers in one area or overall.*

You will also have information about students who are in vulnerable groups:

- *LAC: students/children who are looked after by adults other than their biological parent – perhaps by grandparents or extended family in an unofficial capacity or as a result of a care order, fostered or adopted or charges of the state.*

- *PPI: students in receipt of pupil premium income.*

- *FSM: students entitled to free school meals.*

- *EAL: students for whom English is an additional language.*

- *SEN register: whatever your codes may be, you will generally know who has a statement of special educational needs and who has an educational healthcare plan (EHCP). You will probably also know who has dyslexia, dyspraxia, an attention deficit disorder, an attachment disorder (although many ADs are not diagnosed as such and an AD may only manifest itself in behaviour), social anxiety or other social disorders, visual impairment, hearing impairment, physical impairment. There may be other groups.*

So, equipped with all this data, it then becomes important for a teacher to understand what to do with it. Most important is the need to adjust teaching to meet the needs of those in vulnerable groups whose life chances are affected by their circumstances.

In 2017 data was compiled to show how likely students in certain groups were to achieve entry to higher education, compared with the general population of school students. In comparison to the 38% of students in the general population who went on to higher education, just 6% of looked-after children were able to access university or college. There are similar gaps with other vulnerable groups. Whether or not we believe it's important for students' life chances that they go to university, we can all perhaps accept that everyone should have an equal chance to access higher education and, were this the case, more might choose to go.

There are things we can do as teachers in the classroom to redress the balance and at least help to narrow the gap.

❖ Have a secure understanding of how a range of factors can inhibit pupils' ability to learn, and how best to overcome them

The reason that all of these vulnerable groups are identified by the government and made known to schools is that they are all disadvantaged by certain factors in their history or their present, and these factors are potential obstacles to them maximising their life chances.

One of the tragedies of life is that it is so unequal that potential talent is lost because the owners of that potential are not in a situation where it can be nurtured and brought to fruition, simply because of factors over which they have no control. This is a tragedy on a personal *and* a societal level because for our public life to have access to the best minds and talents, it needs to be able to draw upon a large pool of trained people. And the best people do not come uniquely from the homes where education is valued and potential is spotted and nurtured.

Human beings are fallible and frail, and the young of the species even more so. We have in our care children who are vulnerable to all sorts of hurt that we cannot heal. But, as I've said, as teachers we can equip ourselves with knowledge and strategies which will enable us to do all we can to redress the balance and effect change and development. We are not healthcare professionals, psychologists, psychiatrists or youth justice workers, and nor should we try to be. We should never underestimate what we do in the classroom to help these vulnerable young people just by teaching our subjects in the most effective ways available to us.

It may seem daunting to approach all the problems that affect our young people and see suggested strategies that could be adopted when accommodating them in our classrooms. The good news is that there is a great degree of commonality between the approaches to the different factors that inhibit young people's progress, and therefore when you adopt "best practice" strategies in one area, it is highly likely that they will be of help in others, too.

For instance, there are some simple strategies to help students with dyslexia which can be used by all teachers for all students without much difficulty. Teachers can be helped by school administration in this. Dyslexic students find it easier to read text on a pale blue or yellow background, so why not have a printer-photocopier loaded with pale blue or yellow paper, which would be used by all teachers for all handouts to all students? Would the cost of coloured paper outweigh the costs of having teachers, learning support assistants or teaching assistants printing out different resources for some students, and thereby labelling those students in the eyes of the others (the curse of the coloured worksheets...)? Set up all PowerPoint applications with a default pale blue or yellow background – much easier if you don't even have to think about it. Set Open Dyslexic Font as a default on all resources for students. It is a great help to dyslexic students, rooting the characters on the bottom line, but does not distract other students. These are simple mechanisms that can yield great benefits for some students.

Later, under Those with an Autistic Spectrum Disorder, we will examine ten techniques for use with each of several different vulnerable groups. These are intended for use in classes where you need to consider certain individuals but, as you use the techniques with those individuals, you may well think they are useful for all.

❖ Demonstrate an awareness of the physical, social and intellectual development of children, and know how to adapt teaching to support pupils' education at different stages of development

This is an area that really doesn't need a great deal of explanation. You teach a year 4 class in a different way from the way you teach a year 10 class. You will speak differently, using different language and a different tone. Your material will be differently constructed and there is a certain level of appropriateness to different key stages and year groups.

If we take Sex and Relationship Education, for instance, it goes without saying that the way in which you introduce this in year 7, and what you talk about, will be wholly different from the emphasis in year 11. Although there will be those who are precocious and worldly in year 7, it is wise to err on the side of caution when talking about sex, and although there will be more reticent year 11s, hopefully most of the questions they have been too shy to ask as they progress through school will have been answered and their cumulative knowledge will be age-appropriate by the time they get to the age of 15 or 16.

❖ Have a clear understanding of the needs of all pupils, using distinctive teaching approaches to engage and support them

These groups might include:

Those with special educational needs:

Dyslexia

By far the most common special educational need we will come across in our classroom is dyslexia, which is thought to affect some 4% of the students in our classroom. In other words, it is probable that at least one student in each of your classes will have some level of dyslexia. If they have been identified as dyslexic then you will have this information but bear in mind that some students may not have been diagnosed. For this reason, some schools consider it good practice to use strategies to help students with dyslexia across the board in all their classes.

Educational problems

- *Learning letters and their sounds*
- *Organising letters and words in reading, writing and spelling*
- *Reading for comprehension at normal speed*
- *Understanding written explanations or instructions*
- *Learning a foreign language with different rules and structures*
- *Learning Maths operations*
- *Doing Maths questions*
- Reading quickly enough to comprehend a block of text

Social and emotional problems

- *Poor self-image: students with dyslexia can feel very negative about themselves, thinking they are less clever or less able than their peers. A more progressive attitude to dyslexia should have improved this in recent years, but teachers should recognise this tendency as a factor of the student with dyslexia. They tend to attribute any success to external factors such as "luck" or a "fluke", but see failure as caused by their own "fault" and "stupidity", which can result in less effort if a student starts to wonder what the point is in trying hard. This can obviously lead to associated problems such as the student leaving education early. However, success in school can lead to a much more positive self-image. In other words, teachers can make a real difference to a dyslexic child's life.*
- *Depression: students with dyslexia can be prone to depression and develop negative opinions not only of their own selves but also of their environment and their chances in the future. A positive approach from their teachers and success at school can have a dramatic impact on this negative outlook.*

Teaching students with dyslexia

Teachers need to make interventions to assist students to succeed and to recognise their own success – a key tenet of the Strictly Positive Teacher. Remember that academic success at school can have a transformative effect on the lives of these students, even more than other student groups.

These suggested interventions are reasonable to ask of teachers in all classrooms. The good news is that many of these interventions are good practice whether you are working with students with or without dyslexia.

Interventions involving resources

Students spend much of their day working with resources of one sort or another: exercise books, textbooks, worksheets, online textbooks and websites to name but a few. These resources will not, for the most part, give instructions for differentiation for all the students in your class. So, you will have to plan as far as possible for the success of all using what you have, but tweaking things. Here are some practical suggestions about how to tweak or add to your resources to give your students with dyslexia the best chance of success.

Before class – preparing resources and planning

- *Use Open Dyslexia Font when preparing resources. It is common practice in many schools now to use this as the default font for all resources prepared in-house. If this is not available, use a plain, evenly spaced sans serif font such as Arial or Comic Sans (better with primary!). Alternatives might include Verdana, Tahoma, Century Gothic, Trebuchet.*
- *Using font size 12-14 can be helpful for clarity. Additionally, using larger font sizes and increasing spacing can help separate sections.*
- *When preparing work on PowerPoint or on paper, use a pale colour background. A pastel background such as yellow and blue has been shown to be easier for students with dyslexia than the glare of black text on white. If your school can be persuaded to bulk buy pale yellow or blue paper instead of the standard white, dyslexic students and their parents will recognise that their needs are being met in a positive way.*
- *You may wish to check the readability level of your documents. The way you do this will differ depending on your word-processing software. If you search for "readability" in your tool bar search field, you will find how to do it. Readability will usually be expressed either as a Flesch Reading Ease score, or a Flesch-Kincaid Grade Level Score. The Flesch score is from 1–100; the higher the score, the easier the material. The Flesch-Kincaid expresses a document level as suitable for a particular USA school grade. You should be looking at 70-80 on the Flesch reading ease scale, and around 5.0 on the Flesch-Kincaid scale. (To give you an idea, the script of the work in progress of this*

book is currently rated as 63.3 on the Flesch scale, and as 8.7 on the Flesch-Kincaid scale.)

- *Use left-justified with ragged right edge. (No differentiated margins.)*
- *Avoid narrow newspaper-style columns (as used in newspapers).*
- *Lines should not be too long – ideally, 60 to 70 characters.*
- *Avoid cramping material and using long, dense paragraphs: space it out. Line spacing of 1.5 is preferable.*
- *Avoid starting a sentence at the end of a line.*
- *Use bullet points and numbering rather than continuous prose.*
- *Highlight essential information. If an adolescent can read a regular textbook but has difficulty finding the essential information, the teacher can mark this information with a highlight pen. When emphasising specific text, avoid underlining and italics: these tend to make the words appear to run together. Use bold instead.*
- *AVOID TEXT IN BLOCK CAPITALS: lower case is much easier to read. For headings, use a larger font size in bold, lower case. Boxes and borders can be used for effective emphasis.*
- *Check that written instructions are clear and broken down into manageable chunks. If possible, highlight the key words or phrases in the instructions.*
- *Provide a glossary of vocabulary and key words that are essential for understanding. Avoid asking students to copy lists of words, especially new vocabulary. Ask them to stick pre-prepared lists in their books instead.*
- *Develop reading guides. A reading guide helps the reader understand the main ideas and sort out the numerous details related to the main ideas. A reading guide can be developed paragraph-by-paragraph, page-by-page, or section-by-section.*

In the lesson
- *Present the work to be done in small, staggered amounts. If students are anxious about the amount of work to be done, separating it into chunks will enable them to see how much they have achieved. In this way students won't become anxious or overwhelmed and unable to start.*
- *Work with students to agree a realistic goal. Some students may set unachievable targets for themselves and then regard*

themselves as failures if they don't achieve them. If the goal is a realistic one then teachers can help students to see themselves as succeeding.

- *Block out extraneous stimuli. When reading, a reading ruler, which overlays the white with a pastel colour and focusses on one line of text at a time, can be extremely useful. A student who is distracted by visual stimuli on a sheet may be encouraged to use plain (preferably pastel-coloured) paper to cover extraneous text and images in order to enable them to focus on the critical material. If a student is easily distracted by visual stimuli on a full worksheet or page, a blank sheet of paper can be used to cover sections of the page not being worked on. In addition, windows can be used to display individual math problems.*

- *In exercise books or workbooks, ask students to make a diagonal cut at the lower right-hand corner of the pages they have completed. This makes it easier for them to find their place.*

- *Provide additional practice activities. Some resources do not provide enough practice activities for students with learning problems to become thoroughly confident in selected skills. Even if they do, it is good practice for teachers to have extra exercises available, not only for students with dyslexia, but for all students as reinforcement for mastery. Consider games, reciprocal teaching, IT resources and supplementary worksheets.*

- *Use audio recordings, especially for homework. These can be prepared by the teacher or LSA reading for the students, or by using a text-to-speech programme. There are many available as websites. Directions, stories, and specific lessons can be recorded. The student can replay the tape to clarify understanding of directions or concepts. Also, to improve reading skills, the student can read the printed words silently as they are presented as an audio recording.*

- *Those teachers who use tablets can use any number of apps to record lessons with explanatory text or illustrations and send them to some or all students.*

Those with an Autistic Spectrum Disorder (ASD)

Recently, autism has been elevated to a disorder on its own rather than part of "developmental disability", and terms such as Asperger syndrome have been dropped.

The diagnostic criteria for autism are all about behaviour. There is no blood test or genetic screening which can diagnose an autistic spectrum disorder. The manifest behaviour which leads to a diagnosis of autism has been most recently gathered into two domains:

1. *communication and social interactions; and*

2. *restrictive and repetitive interests and activities, including stereotypy (repetitive or ritualistic motions, actions or utterances without any obvious point) and sensory issues.*

So, what does that mean for teachers? How can we support students with autism?

It may first be useful to look at classroom "problems" from the point of view of the student who is exhibiting them.

- *Student problem 1: inability to understand what a parent, teacher or school wants, and why*
- *Student problem 2: inability to communicate their own needs or desires*
- *Student problem 3: difficulty establishing and maintaining "appropriate" social interaction*
- *Student problem 4: difficulty understanding the consequences of their own behaviour*
- *Student problem 5: the need to engage in repetitive behaviours which may limit their own ability to learn and to get on with peers*

Teachers may have different problems:
- *Teacher problem 1: student is non-compliant with classroom rules and routines*
- *Teacher problem 2: student becomes agitated and argumentative when things do not go their way*
- *Teacher problem 3: student may destroy work or property*

- *Teacher problem 4: student may become verbally or physically aggressive*

The educational interventions most likely to have a successful outcome with students with autism are those which aim to develop positive and pro-social behaviours.

Because the autistic spectrum spans such a wide range of symptoms and behaviours, any successful approach to a student will be supported by a school-wide protocol, which ensures all teachers understand the student's specific needs.

This will include notes about:
- *The student's diagnosis*
- *Their communication and social skills*
- *What the young person does well*
- *What they struggle with*
- *What is liable to upset them – anxiety triggers*
- *What is likely to motivate them – their favourite activities*

Equipped with this knowledge, the Strictly Positive Classroom Teacher can then tailor their own behaviour and their behaviour management, as well as their teaching, to offer the young person the best chance of success in their lesson.

Here are some ways in which you can help students with ASD:

1. *Establish contact with parents and ensure they know that you are doing your best to support their child. Parents want to establish a cooperative working relationship with teachers. You will need them to support you – you need to know how to work best with the student, and they are the experts on their child. For all concerned this communication is key.*

2. *Seating: ask the student where they would be most comfortable sitting – organise broadly around them. Do not change seating plans without warning – this may cause anxiety and result in behaviour issues.*

3. *Give instructions in lists, chunking information down. Consider writing this down, either on a Post-it® or a mini-whiteboard, as a*

prompt. Provide some starting points for tasks: vocabulary, structures or ideas.

4. *Share the lesson plan with the TA or LSA if the student has one. Indicate in advance where you may ask the student a question so they can be prepared. If there is no one to assist the student, try to avoid putting them on the spot by asking them a question publicly, without warning.*

5. *Try to use the student's interest to harness their attention or use visuals. Verbal information is fleeting for some students with ASD, so something visual which they can refer to will help.*

6. *Watch your own behaviour. Try to communicate as clearly and economically as possible without allegory, subtext, irony or jokes. When problems occur, whether or not they involve the students with ASD, try to employ positive behaviour management and avoid raising your voice or shouting, which will almost certainly exacerbate behaviour issues.*

7. *Understand the student's behaviour: remember that behaviour is often communicating a need, anxiety or difficulty. This may be around one of the following concerns:*

8. *Do they understand what you mean? What they need to do?*

9. *Is it about peer interactions?*

10. *Are they over-stimulated? Maybe the class is too noisy, too unruly, or there is too much going on…*

11. *Are they worried, anxious, fearful?*

12. *Have high expectations: read specific advice about teaching your subject to students with ASD. Try and build positive relationships with them. Remember, some problems that are typical of the condition can mask high ability.*

13. *Check in every so often to make sure they are on track. But be respectful of their personal space and don't make or insist on eye contact.*

14. *Differentiate homework: many autistic students are exhausted after a day at school due to the demands of coping with the stress and anxiety of constant stimulation and interaction. Others have rigid ideas about the separation of school and*

home – school is for schoolwork and home is not where you do schoolwork. Reduce or compress the work set to minimise difficulty in getting work done, or try to find a way to relate homework to students' interests, if possible.

Those of high ability

We are probably all aware of the ways in which some notable figures in history have been dismissed early in their lives. Little Albert may have been overlooked by his teachers at primary school as he only started to speak at four years old and couldn't read until he was seven – how surprised must they have been when he became famous as Albert Einstein, the renowned physicist and a byword for genius. Young Thomas Edison, whose brain was described by his teacher as "addled", surprised all by becoming one of the great inventors of the modern age. A student described in his school report as "Hopeless. Certainly on the road to failure," went on to become John Lennon. Mary Leakey, later a renowned paleoanthropologist, was repeatedly excluded from her convent school.

While these anecdotes are amusing and provide encouragement to those students who struggle in school, what if we consider all the Alberts, Thomases, Johns and Marys who did not have the same resilience, who did not persist in the pursuit of their passions? What would the world have lost if Einstein, Edison, Lennon and Leakey had bought into their teachers' low judgement of them? How much has the world already lost because teachers and schools have written off others who may have made equally world-changing contributions?

Identifying those of high ability is trickier than identifying those who need more help. Too many schools rely on data, but many children may be falsely identified in this way. One of the characteristics of a gifted child, for instance, is that faced with a simple question they may seek deeper meaning and thereby make mistakes. There is also the fact that different schools and different teachers are able to effect significantly different results for their students in blanket tests.

There are some general identifiers, such as:
- *Curiosity*
- *Intellectual playfulness*
- *The ability to grasp concepts quickly*

- *The ability to extrapolate easily from concrete examples to general rules*
- *Becoming absorbed by a question, rather than giving up*
- *Questioning*

But individual departments will have their own means of identifying able and gifted students.

For example, a Maths department may look for students who:
- *Grasp the formal structure of a question*
- *Recognise pattern*
- *Can specialise and make conjectures*
- *Think flexibly and adopt problem-solving approaches*
- *Reason logically*
- *Are able to generalise from examples*
- *Can work backwards and forwards when solving a problem*
- *Remember mathematical relationships, problem types, ways of approaching a problem and patterns of reasoning*

A Geography department may identify as gifted students who:
- *Are intrigued by the workings of their own environments*
- *Analyse confidently and draw conclusions*
- *Design creatively and interpret spatial representation*
- *Formulate opinions and use evidence to support their own views*
- *Enjoy and can use confidently a wide range of visual resources, including maps and photographs*
- *Are enthusiastic observers of the world around them*

Art teachers notice students who:
- *Analyse and interpret their observations and present them creatively*
- *Are enthusiastic and interested in the visual world*
- *Can sustain concentration, constantly refining ideas*
- *Draw on existing knowledge, make connections and draw on comparisons with others' work*
- *Enjoy experimenting with materials and are able to go beyond the conventional*
- *Use confidently a wide range of skills and techniques*

Most teachers in their own departments will have a range of similar criteria which they use to identify gifted and talented students.

Does high ability mean a student has a special educational need? Absolutely! If we are to teach all students to the limit of their potential then it is no more acceptable to make only one educational diet available to our gifted students than it is to have only one diet available for our more vulnerable students. No one would think of failing to differentiate for students who need more help; why should they not differentiate for students who need more challenge?

According to research conducted by the Sutton Trust the risks of not recognising and nurturing particular talent is great. Able students who are not engaged and challenged can become bored and disruptive and once they are recognised as poorly behaved that is what teachers notice rather than their potential ability. From there a vicious cycle starts, where they are less challenged, become less engaged, more disruptive and so on. While most research illustrates that most crimes are committed by people with lower measured IQs, there have been studies that look at the significant number of prisoners who are highly gifted. That research suggested highly gifted people experience more isolation, bullying and difficulty in forming attachments, factors which may predispose a person to criminal behaviour. It was said some years ago, anecdotally, that there was a higher percentage of gifted individuals incarcerated than in the general populace. Imagine how much benefit to society is lost if this is true!

Teachers should be aware therefore that some behaviours displayed in a classroom and interpreted as signs that a student is challenging, annoying or rebellious may actually be showing evidence of unrecognised intellectual giftedness. These students may correct their teachers, question your rules and policies, giving reasons why they are inadequate. They may have inconsistent work habits, exhibit poor self-control, be nakedly direct in their interactions with their teacher and have mood swings; they may be over-competitive and stand up for themselves and their convictions when corrected. These behaviours are not always signs of giftedness, but teachers should consider whether or not they are masking something unexpected.

So you have identified the gifted students in your room, whether at departmental level, or a school-wide identification – what do you do next?

At this point things become a little more blurred in terms of what teachers should do in their own classrooms. There are a wide variety of approaches, and what follows is just a selection of general suggestions. Remember, as a Strictly Positive Teacher you are trying to *a)* recognise the child for having the special need that they do; and *b)* to take action to do what is in your power to enable them to progress towards their own potential, as distinct from the needs of the class.

It would be difficult to stipulate ways in which the gifted students in our classes should have differentiated work, but there are certain general pointers that we could heed:

- Bloom's Taxonomy: it is wise to employ a flexible approach to thinking about learning when considering the needs of gifted students. Creating tasks which build on the higher-order learning skills will assist these students. These tasks might be built around:
  - Creating
    - What would happen if…?
    - Is there another way to…?
  - Evaluating
    - How do you know that…?
    - On what grounds can you justify…?
    - Why would you make that decision?
    - What are the arguments for and against…?
  - Remembering
    - Make a list of …
    - Write an account of…
    - Summarise…
  - Understanding
    - Discuss this from the point of view of…
    - Explain the differences between…

- How would this affect…?
- What were the results of this…?

   o   Applying

- How does this rule apply to…?
- How would you use this to…?
- Conduct an experiment to prove…?

   o   Analysing

- What was the overall plan…?
- How do the elements combine…?
- What is the general rule?

- *Have extra work handy when students are working on mastering a particular learning point. Extra here does not just mean more; it means work which stretches the learning point by adding an extra layer of challenge, something that will engage the learner by offering them something they cannot immediately do. Use of the kind of tasks suggested as part of the higher-order learning skills of Bloom's Taxonomy is helpful here. Awakening a student's curiosity is the best way to absorb them in their learning. Many of us may have met a student who causes chaos throughout school except in a subject where he or she excels. That annoying kid isn't seen in Maths, where he's regarded as only just short of being a genius. He loves Maths and wants his Maths teacher's approbation, because he knows he can get it. In other lessons the only way he can get attention is by playing up.*
- *Ask students to create learning questions about the material. To test the depth of knowledge of an individual, ask them to manipulate the material to create extra questions which could be asked. Start with extra questions at the end of a task, and then add something additional to be solved.*
- *Clarify learning and acknowledge expertise by asking a gifted student to take a student who is finding an exercise or piece of work difficult. This should not be an ongoing stratagem, using*

the gifted student as an extra resource in the classroom; instead, the teacher can help the gifted student to clarify and refine their own thinking about something by breaking it down into component parts and teaching it to another.

- *Make available extension reading material – include on your Virtual Learning Environment or in your subject handbook extension reading sources for each topic (sub-topic if possible). Invite students to discuss them if they have further questions.*
- *Make available extra activities outside school. There is a range of activities provided by external agencies, from writing competitions, to public speaking opportunities, to Maths challenges, to engineering projects. Simply recognising a student and proposing such activities to them can be a hugely effective way of encouraging and stimulating a student with a gift. If a teacher can see beyond the disruptive behaviour of a naughty gifted chid, the change effected can be even more transformational, not only on behaviour but on a child's self-image.*

Those with English as an additional language

This group encompasses individuals with extremely different experiences, from the student who, although she speaks another language at home, has been in the UK education system for years, through the asylum seeker who has a basic working knowledge of several languages, to the refugee who has been in the country a matter of weeks and comes to your Physics class with no English at all.

As with any other student in your class, the first thing to do is to discover exactly what your EAL students do know, so that you can properly assist. The quality and quantity of information which comes to teachers before they meet their students varies from school to school, but make use of as much as you can and ask for more if you need it, understanding that it may not exist.

This guidance is intended for teachers welcoming new arrivals, with little English, to their classroom. It will, however, be useful for any student who does not have expertise in English.

1. *Speak and write: to assist students with little English, writing down instructions, tasks or key words will be very useful. Even classroom language can usefully be displayed in this way, perhaps with illustrations. Ensure that this information remains visible. This will be helpful to the whole of the class, but particularly to the student who cannot easily remember the key vocabulary of the lesson you're teaching. It will also allow them to participate in the lesson, which is key to making them feel included in your classroom and with the other students.*

2. *Use visual resources: it will be very useful for an EAL student to have visual representations of the learning where possible, to assist them where the verbal or written input is not sufficient to help them comprehend. This may not always be possible but is worth considering if you can provide it.*

3. *Provide scaffolding for extended tasks with sentence starters and a word-bank to help them cope.*

4. *Provide dictionaries: English-English dictionaries could be provided on tables. Make a judgement about whether you allow the student to use translation dictionaries. This will depend on the nature of the task and the character and needs of the student. Some teachers want to limit students to the use of English, which will help them work things out in the language. Others allow students a crutch in the form of the ability to translate.*

5. *Build in group work: it may be that a student may be nervous about asking for assistance in an open class environment, and thereby drawing attention to himself, but he may be confident enough to practise language or ask for help in the unthreatening environment of a group task, especially when buddied up with a helpful peer.*

6. *After the first couple of lessons, pre-teach where possible: at the end of each lesson, supply the student with material for the next lesson, either in the form of a handout or supplied electronically. This way the student may be able to look it over and prepare alone or with a parent or carer, and they will feel empowered when they return to your classroom.*

7. *Be respectful of shyness: there is often a phase when a new student is making sense of the torrent of language in a school environment, working out the meanings of the different registers of language around them, from peers and teachers and in the textbooks and study resources available to them. Often a student will wait to speak until they are confident that their utterance will be perfect. This necessitates a lot of silent concentration and effort and is a normal stage in new language acquisition. Try not to make a student speak until they're confident to do so.*

8. *Learn something about culture backgrounds: if you show that you have bothered to look into the background of your students, you show that you have respect for them and see them as whole people with knowledge and experience they cannot yet express.*

9. *But don't make the student the spokesperson for a whole culture: if a student has come from a war-torn country, don't ask them to describe or give an opinion about it. For one thing, they may not have experience of some of the aspects of that country's heritage which you have read about or seen on the news, but in addition it may be painful to discuss – and anyway, they may not have the language to discuss it.*

10. *Do not confuse language difficulties with lack of intelligence: try to see beyond the struggle to express ideas and concepts to what the student is trying to say, either in spoken or written language. They are trying to do two jobs here, and take on two learning loads. Be careful to separate how they're doing in each.*

Those with Attachment Disorders

There are many factors that can bring about an Attachment Disorder in a child, but a cursory glance at its contributory factors shows how important it is that teachers have some knowledge of the existence of Attachment Disorders and recognise the importance of giving children and young people the right amount of the right type of attention.

Among the causes are:

- o Separation from the primary caregiver
    - o Divorce or separation
    - o Parental imprisonment
    - o Parental addiction or substance abuse
    - o Parental depression
    - o Bereavement
    - o Change in the primary caregiver
    - o Fostering
    - o Adoption
- o Neglect
- o Abuse
- o Perceived abandonment
- o Frequent moves
- o Traumatic experiences
- o Undiagnosed painful illness such as colic, ear infections etc
- o Lack of attunement between parent and child

This is a long but not exhaustive list. In summary, anything that ruptures the natural, ongoing bond between parent and child can cause anxiety, wariness and sometimes shame in children and young people, and can cause them problems. These problems can manifest themselves in behaviours which may include:

- o Incessant chatter
- o Incessant questions
- o Lack of impulse control
- o Being inappropriately clingy or demanding
- o Indiscriminate affection towards strangers

- Being intensely argumentative
- Defiance and anger
- A lack of eye contact, except when lying
- Hypervigilance
- Hyperactivity
- Learning lags or delay
- Being manipulative – superficially charming and engaging
- Poor peer relationships
- Dishonesty
- Cruelty
- Physical aggression
- Destruction of property
- Destructive to self or others
- Lack of conscience

We can see that attachment disorders manifest themselves in a variety of behaviours ranging from the low-level annoyance and disruption that emerges in most classes from time to time, to serious behaviours which must be tackled at a higher level in the school community.

We know that in modern society a great number of the ills, separately or together, affect a great many of the young people in our care. Most of us will recognise common problems that we experience in our classrooms as possible pointers to some degree of attachment disorder. It makes sense then to adopt strategies that work to address these issues, and apply them to all our students in all our classrooms to try to help students as best we can to access learning.

The crucial thing is that when we meet students with these issues, whether or not we are aware of them, we have to set the expectations for the way in which communication will be managed in our classrooms.

"Behaviour is communication." I have seen these words attributed to several educationalists and child development experts, but I heard it from

Louise Bombér, who speaks and writes brilliantly on the subject of Attachment Disorder. Communication is not only spoken or written; by everything a student does they are telling us who they are and how they feel. Those silent young people who surprise when they hand in work which shows they have fully engaged with the teaching communicate as much as the student who struggles with the work and responds by channelling his effort into distracting the rest of the class so that his perceived failure will not be noticed.

And so it is completely understandable that within minutes, seconds even in some cases, we can see the level of need demonstrated. Many of the kind of behaviours you will observe in your lessons from children with Attachment Disorders (diagnosed or undiagnosed) will be the behaviours of toddlers who have not been able to progress past the stage of being needy and clingy, hungry for attention from the person who they are not sure will provide it. In your classroom that person is you, and this can be very irritating when you have thirty students in the class and a lot to get though. Using Strictly Positive behaviour management in this situation will obviously be of great use, and there are other strategies you can adopt, too.

The most important thing to remember is that this student has, in this attention-seeking behaviour, not progressed beyond the toddler stage. So when you are considering how to work with this student, think toddler.

So, how specifically can you help the child with an Attachment Disorder in your class?

Recognise stress points

- o Running out of time is perceived as failure, which can lead the student to give up and become disengaged or disruptive – provide a timer or stopwatch, or direct them to look at the clock and give regular time updates, so they are crystal clear about the time they have left.

- o Being interrupted and moved onto a new activity – students with unsafe attachments can feel that their teacher has forgotten about them. Check in with the student and arrange a way to help them catch up. Let them know you haven't forgotten them.

- Waiting: if something has been promised, it must happen – these children have been let down many times. If you're seeing to someone else in your classroom, acknowledge the hand up and say you'll be over next. Then see that student next.

- Be aware that for students who already feel abandoned, any staff changes equal further abandonment. Be sensitive about staff absence, changes of teacher or LSA or moving to another class. Make sure students don't feel it's personal.

Before admitting students into the classroom

- Set the tone for the lesson. Smile, greet the child by name, maybe give them a thumbs up – let them know (not too obviously) that everything is going to be okay.

- Make your expectations clear, but concise – think toddler.

Upon entry

- Seating: position students with Attachment Disorders near the door, with backs to the wall – they can scan the room and know there is no unseen danger.

- Notice anything they get right – sitting down promptly, having the right equipment, taking their coat off – they gain a sense of worth and belonging, and become more ready to learn.

- Explicitly and calmly state (and restate, and restate) rules and expectations – think toddler.

- Have spare equipment ready – pick your battles and don't get dragged into conflict.

In the lesson

- Use positive language – "put your hand up" instead of "don't call out" – toddlers' brains focus on individual words.

- State instructions clearly and simply and add an explanation of the reason for it – think toddler.

- Wonder aloud – "I wonder if you're feeling a bit lost..."; "I wonder if you would be able to try this exercise..." Give them a safe way to express difficulty or an unchallenging target to aim for.

- o Use language of choice – give them some sense of control. "If you choose to chat when you should be drawing your graph, I will have to put your name on the negative side."

- o Keep noticing and commending appropriate behaviour, but be specific; they need to recognise that you're sincere, so instead of "well done!" say, "You've drawn that graph really neatly – well done for using a ruler!" You cannot praise too much, as long as you're praising specifics.

- o If you promise to help, remember. If you say "I'm just helping Johnny, I'll be there in a minute", go over immediately after you help Johnny – waiting causes problems. Toddlers again.

- o If you promise a reward, follow through. If you say "I'll give you a house point", put it on the system – they will feel let down, again, if you don't.

Upon leaving your classroom

- o Give them a good memory. Smile, use their name with a positive comment – let them remember that they had a good lesson with you.

A WORD ABOUT CONTROL BATTLES

- o Do not try and address all perceived problems at once. This is doomed to failure. The child will be overloaded with shame and failure and will respond by fighting, fleeing or freezing.

- o Pick your battles. Some things are more important than others. Know when not to notice in the greater good.

- o When conflict looks near try to deflect it with humour, but avoid sarcasm at all times.

- o If you are driven to threaten a sanction, follow through if you need to – consistency is important.

When things go wrong

- o You might try first of all to keep students in class; use "time in" – if space and furniture allow: have a chair set up somewhere in the class where a student can continue with studies.

- o Time out – let students have a specific period of time to calm down, but organise "time out" cards for them. This should not be something which is done in an uncontrolled way.

- o Partner classrooms are a good arrangement – colleagues in adjacent or nearby classrooms should agree to accommodate students where necessary. This can be timetabled and timetables kept easily available. Students should be sent with enough appropriate work, and should return it to their teacher at the end of the lesson.

- o If things are really going wrong, call upon a person who is very familiar to the child to take them out.

Serious incidents

- o Involve one person – preferably a key adult – who is neutral. Avoid raising anxiety as it risks making behaviour worse.

- o Stay connected with the child – don't make them feel abandoned.

- o Provide reparation opportunity asap.

- o After reparation, reassure the child that the relationship is not damaged.

In short:

Raise level of security; reduce level of anxiety

Build relationships

Raise level of trust; reduce feeling of abandonment

Think toddler

Those with Attention Disorders

There can be hardly a teacher out there who has not encountered students who exhibit the signs of an Attention Disorder with or without the hyperactivity element. There are many people whose ADD or ADHD is being diagnosed in adulthood, and they are relieved to find there was a reason for the symptoms which afflicted them and made school so difficult for them.

A moment's reflection will remind you that all the things we expect students to do in school are the things students with Attention Disorders find incredibly challenging. They have to sit still, pay attention, listen carefully, follow instructions, concentrate for long periods. Their difficulties manifest themselves in many identifiable ways.

The symptoms include:

- o Distractibility
- o Forgetfulness
- o Inability to concentrate for long periods of time
- o Difficulty learning new material
- o Difficulty listening to instruction
- o Become easily bored
- o Difficulty following instructions
- o Slow processing speed
- o Daydreaming
- o Losing things

The symptoms of hyperactivity may include:

- o Squirming in seat
- o Constant moving and talking
- o Need to touch things or pick them up
- o Insomnia

Symptoms of an impulsiveness element:

- o Calling out without thinking

- o Making inappropriate comments

- o Interrupting

- o Inability to wait their turn

- o Inability to delay gratification

- o Acting without thinking

Obviously, not every child who displays these behaviours suffers from an Attention Disorder but many students, probably the ones whose names are well-known to the staff, may indeed be helped by using strategies for teachers who teach students with such disorders, whether or not they have been diagnosed.

So how can a teacher make it easier for a student with an attention deficit to learn?

1. *Seating: seat students with Attention Disorders away from the distractions provided by windows and doors, preferably right in front of your desk or the area from which you teach so that you are the natural main focus. Avoid having the student facing other students who will be in their eyeline and will thereby distract them, deliberately or accidentally, from you and the work you are teaching or setting. When doing tests, seat students at a desk on their own facing the wall, so as to avoid any distraction; make sure they understand that you are doing this to afford them the best chance of success.*

2. *Instructions: break down instructions into chunks and be prepared to repeat as required. You may wish to have a mini-whiteboard on the student's desk and jot down instructions for the student, so you can redirect their attention to them as you pass by their desk.*

3. *Use visuals: charts, pictures and colour coding all engage attention and may help the student to focus on material you are working with.*

4. ***Encourage students to take notes in their own notebooks***: suggest note-taking proformas: If you create a blank form divided into sections such as questions, ideas, details, anecdotes, and allow students to populate these areas with what seems important to them, and what grabs them, they may start to recognise how they can best assimilate learning.

5. ***Long-term projects***: break down projects into segments, each with success criteria and a completion goal. Accept and mark partial work as it comes in to sustain interest.

6. ***Frequent short tests/quizzes***: assess where possible through a series of short tests rather than one long one. This may not be possible – but if your course of work is assessed through end-of-unit tests, try and ensure students sit these tests at the beginning of a school day so that students with attention problems are fresher and more likely to succeed. (Difficult if you see them once a week in the last period on a Thursday, I know!)

7. ***Use aural cues***: egg timers, service bells, cowbells or horns will be arresting and can draw attention to key points in a lesson. Be very careful not to use these aural cues too often or you'll find that students completely ignore them. It's like the dog owner who is always shouting the dog's name: "Fluffy! Fluffy! Come here, Fluffy! Sit, Fluffy! Down, Fluffy! Fluffy, LEAVE!" After a while all dogs and students hear is white noise.

8. ***Vary activities and pace***: you may find that competitive games and activities suit these students. Stir and settle. It's good practice for all and reduces the chance that your student with ADD will lose focus and become distracted.

9. ***Allow sensory breaks***: it may be that your school day is a number of short 30–40 minute lessons, in which case the transition between lessons will probably provide the sensory breaks which students need to be able to refocus. However, if your lessons are longer, consider incorporating sensory breaks into your classroom practice. A short activity incorporating movement may perform this function, but perhaps allow students to squeeze a rubber ball or other tactile object, or ask them to give out or collect in books. Be careful which fidget toys you choose. I bought some tangle fidget toys, which are composed of several

interconnected pieces. Isaac in year 8 spent every lesson taking them to bits and then would hand the detritus to me as he left the room, as did every student I gave them to. Those of us who remember the 2017 summer of the Fidget Spinner know that if not carefully managed a sensory device can become the focus of the entire lesson, so beware!

10. ***Summarise key points***: *at the end of a lesson summarise, as concisely as possible, the key learning points. Ask three students to repeat them. Do the same with homework. Then get the whole class to repeat the homework together. As much iteration as possible is the name of the game here.*

9

STRICTLY POSITIVE ASSESSMENT

When it comes to the stresses and strains that adversely affect a young person's mental health, official assessment, exams, and parental and school expectations rank near the top of most lists. However, assessment is an absolutely key part of the teaching cycle, and is certainly not something any teacher can hope or even wish to dispense with. This means that the Strictly Positive Teacher, who is trying at all times to have a positive effect on the mental health of the young people in his or her care, must think very carefully about balancing the need for careful and rigorous assessment with the need to protect students' mental health.

Luckily, this is not as difficult as it might at first appear. First, there are as many ways of assessing progress and attainment as there are to skin a cat, and not all of them need to be visible to the student. Yes, a student needs to know how they are doing and what is expected of them, but this doesn't have to be couched in comparison with their peers. Yes, those who are excelling need to be applauded, and in this situation I'm all in favour of public celebration, but equally to be admired and celebrated is the rate of progress: some students will make sudden progress from a low starting point, and this should be seized upon and applauded. Key here is catching them doing it right, a key tenet of Strictly Positive Teaching.

But much of the day-to-day assessment is low-stakes, private assessment in the shape of assessment for learning and marking, and here considerable impact can be made in a wholly supportive and constructive way. I understand why, as part of a discussion on teacher workload, many professionals are questioning the need for, or the efficacy of, marking but I believe it to be one of the most important things that we do.

❖ Know and understand how to assess the relevant subject and curriculum areas, including statutory assessment requirements

Obviously, it is a key part of the work of a head of department to ensure all members of the department are up-to-date with the current subject curriculum areas, and to advise of any changes and discussions around this.

❖ Make use of formative and summative assessment to secure pupils' progress

Assessment for Learning

So, for instance, if you ask students to indicate by a show of hands how fully they think they have met the "I can..." learning objective on the board, where five fingers is "100%" and two fingers is "not very confident", make sure all students have their hands up (although a reluctance to put a hand up also speaks volumes), really look at that forest of hands to check what the overall confidence level of the class is, and where the weakest students are. (Be aware of the propensity of some to go with the majority so as not to show themselves up. If there are students who regularly look around the room before putting up their four fingers, then that's probably telling in itself.)

If they are all quite confident, and even the normally weak students are showing four or five fingers, you can reflect that in your feedback: "Okay, it looks as if you're all relatively confident so I think we'll move on in the next lesson, but if you do have any concerns, don't worry – we'll be going back over this anyway."

If, however, there are a number of students who have definitely not mastered what you're teaching, acknowledge that and be accountable for it: "Right, I definitely need to think of other ways of explaining this to you. Don't worry – we'll do a bit more work on it next time. Those of you who do feel like you've got it, we can find some way of going into it a bit more deeply for you."

In other words, if most or all of the students feel they have successfully learned the material, then you can congratulate yourself that you, as a teacher, have enabled them to make progress; if most of them declare that they're not confident, then be accountable – the method of teaching you chose has not been fully successful and you need to think of another way of embedding the message. Remember that in the Strictly Positive model failure is part of the progress. Not everything works first time, and it is wise to acknowledge that and not beat yourself up about it. Don't be that teacher who, faced with a classroom full of students who haven't understood what they have tried to teach, turns on them and blames them for their "inability" to get it. The rule is: if a few students don't get it, you can give them a little extra help to nudge them into comprehension; if most of the class don't get it, it was probably the teaching that was the problem. It happens to all of us. We just have to adjust.

It goes without saying that it's always a good idea to have some enrichment or challenge material available for those who are always ahead of the rest. Students who are bored can be disruptive or lose focus and go backwards in their learning. Maybe you can use them to do some peer-teaching. Teaching material to a peer who does not yet understand it makes the able students really focus on the essence of the subject matter.

Summative Assessment

In whatever form it takes, summative assessment is an opportunity for students to show off what they have learned, and a chance to gain recognition for attainment or progress.

As far as summative assessment goes, it is very important that when teachers are feeding back on tests or end-of-unit assessments, the students who have made the most progress from a low starting point are given praise in the same way as those who have achieved full marks. What is important is always that the student is making progress, and they need to understand that. If it is attainment that always attracts praise or reward, then those who start off by under-performing in their first module, unit or topic might simply stop trying as they will never get credit like the top performing students.

I would advise that assessment be carried out regularly. It is more engaging for students if different types of assessment are used on a regular basis so that the students become used to a varied diet of activities, and don't see these activities as boring same-old tests. But, even if they are, they can always be sold as an opportunity for the students to show what they have learned. Having said that, whatever form these tests take, they should be rigorous and the ensuing judgements should be secure. Sharing feedback in as thorough but anonymous a way as possible ensures that students see the purpose of what you are measuring and why.

So, whether you do a vocabulary test on a scrap of paper after learning homework, or you ask students to list ten features of coastal regions, or invite them to record a presentation on a historical figure or time, the assessments should visibly reflect the content of what you have taught them.

In key stage four and five do not presume that after you spent hours devising ways of teaching a certain topic to your students, they will retain all that knowledge when you have left the topic. It is wise to revisit a topic of the curriculum that you have already completed in the middle of the following topic in order to ensure that what you thought the students had learned, they have indeed learned. In this way, students understand that learning is not a temporary thing, but a process, and everything that is taught needs to be retained for the examination at the end of their studies.

❖ Use relevant data to monitor progress, set targets and plan subsequent lessons

Some of us hate data and question its usefulness – others, like me, are data queens and kings. What we would all agree with is that teachers can only go so far in using data to monitor progress, set targets and plan subsequent lessons. The problem with data is that there is no column for *life*.

❖ Give pupils regular feedback, both orally and through accurate marking

To my mind assessment is for teachers and students. It can be usefully given to heads of department and faculty and senior leaders, but that is not who it's for. For that reason it is essential that teachers supply feedback to students as part of the assessment cycle. In fact, a large part of the point of assessment is feedback. How many teachers will give a grade without feedback on that grade? Yes, it is a fact that when students receive a grade and comment many will ignore the comment and see only the grade. For that reason it is arguably more sensible and useful to give students comments only, while noting grades in mark books.

❖ Encourage pupils to respond to the feedback

The key word here is *encourage*. This has been misinterpreted by too many schools as *require*. I am generally in favour of a system which routinely invites students to reflect and comment upon the feedback they receive, but I am opposed to any activity which is made mandatory, because it is then done for its own sake, whether that is teachers being required to ask questions of students as part of the assessment process, or students being required to respond to largely pointless questions, and then sanctioned by teachers who have better things to do when those students don't respond.

But it is essential that we do encourage students to reflect upon what they're being advised to do – do they know how to achieve it? Do they know what the teacher means by their comments? How are they going to achieve it? What will success look like? These are the questions we can ask to encourage students to reflect upon their assessment and the ensuing feedback. Will they do this without being *required* to do this? Will they learn more if they're forced into written responses, which the teacher will tick to confirm the circle has been closed?

Most schools will have their own policies about how to encourage students to respond to feedback, and clearly teachers must conform to the requirements of these policies, but it is important that teachers find their own ways of making this learning dialogue worthwhile and meaningful to both student and teacher.

10

STRICTLY POSITIVE PROFESSIONAL COLLABORATION AND COOPERATION

Many of the positive effects of school on the mental health of students and teachers and the cohesiveness of an educational community stem from the sense that everyone in the school community is engaged on a common mission, which is to provide learning for students in a healthy, friendly, cooperative, collaborative environment.

Every school has its ambiance, something a visitor can sense just by spending time around the site. A cursory glance around can convey all sorts of messages. Teachers and students greeting one another with a smile, rather than scurrying past each other, heads down, each pretending not to notice the other – this speaks volumes to a guest of the school. Members of the community knowing one another's names is always something to look out for, although obviously it is a great deal easier for everyone to know each other by name in a school of 500 students than one of 1500. A sense of a community working together to a common end is something palpable.

One of the great things about the teaching profession is that it is one where there are many opportunities for even the most junior teacher to take an active part in turning the school into a community. The opportunity to rise through the ranks is often cited as a great advantage of the profession, and so it is, but so are the many ways in which a professional can get involved in the softer side of the teaching game – working with other teachers and support professionals as well as students to help improve the environment for all.

❖ Make a positive contribution to the wider life and ethos of the school

Tutoring

It always seems strange to me that there is no obvious or explicit guidance within the teaching standards for Pastoral Leadership and Tutoring. There can be few schools which do not think very, very carefully about the pastoral care of the young people in their community. This is one of the big challenges of teaching in the UK. Whereas in some European countries the job of teacher is limited to imparting subject knowledge and all pastoral care is left to parents, here in Britain looking after our children is an important part of the job of every teacher. Whether or not you believe this is a desirable aspect of British education, it doesn't look as if anything is going to change any time soon. Every time there is some social ill which rises to the forefront of public consciousness, usually as a result of some outrage, atrocity or tragedy, there are calls for schools to make room in their busy schedules to teach British values, or the dangers of radicalisation, or sexting, or self-harming, or drug-taking, or online grooming, or FGM or the importance of personal hygiene, or just saying please and thank you. There are very few areas of a young person's life that are not considered part of their school's remit.

Everybody needs someone who has the responsibility of looking after them. Teachers really need someone – the Head of Department or Line Manager should perform this function and should be responsible not only for the professional performance of a teacher, and their career development, but also their mental and emotional well-being. Also available in many schools are professionals trained as Mental Health First Aiders who will offer support and assistance in case things start to go awry. (This was the government's recent response to the explosion of mental health problems in schools – train more MHFAs. I'm a MHFA. I had two days' training, and I know a few basics and how to signpost available healthcare to my colleagues. It's something but it's not enough.) Trainee teachers and newly qualified colleagues should also have access to a committed mentor. I qualify this with the word "committed" because as the mentor in our department for several years I have heard some appalling stories about what passes for mentoring in other schools.

For our young people, we provide tutors. The job of a tutor is 100% fundamental to the well-being of a young person in their school. To have an adult who meets you every day, for however many minutes, who has an overall view of how you are doing in school, academically, socially and emotionally, is an extraordinary privilege which is afforded our young people, and they probably don't realise what an enormous benefit it can be to them. To be a good tutor doesn't really have to demand a great deal of a teacher unless you have a prescribed and burdensome job description. Teachers probably report in their capacity as a tutor to a pastoral middle leader, probably a Head of Year, Head of Section or Head of House, however your structure is organised. But there do exist some misapprehensions.

As a tutor your prime responsibility is not to take the register and hand out replacement timetables. Your responsibility as a Strictly Positive Tutor is to create positive relationships with your students and be generally aware of what is going on in the lives of those in your form or tutor group. Your prime responsibility is to notice. It should be a different relationship to those which students have with their other teachers. It should be ongoing, supportive, open and, insofar as is possible, non-judgemental. There are plenty of adults who will judge anything a student does. The student will never open up to these adults to air a concern or share a misdemeanour − or worse − that they can't tell their parents about. Sometimes a young person will feel confident enough about the relationship to use a tutor to tell a parent something they don't feel able to share themselves. This can be tricky, too, because sometimes the problem the student has can be with another member of staff − or that is what they will claim. Obviously, you have to use your judgement in such a situation, but a rush to condemn what they say as nonsense is probably not conducive to your relationship with the child. But neither is it a professional course of action to side with the child against your colleague and sympathise too vocally. It is possible to proceed with caution on the line between these two mistakes, but that caution is vital.

How much you feel confident to do, as a tutor, is something you should consider ahead of time. One thing you should remember is that the job of tutor is one that has been allocated to you. You may not choose to be a tutor − it may be a role that comes to you as a corollary of accepting a position as a PE teacher, for instance. You may not feel equipped to take an active role in the pastoral management of students, particularly those who come to you with a history of problems, trauma and difficult behaviour. You may not be comfortable talking to students about personal problems or quizzing them about rumours you may have heard. Presumably, as a tutor you report to a pastoral middle leader. This person probably applied for this role and was appointed because they have some skills in this area and an appetite for getting stuck into the hinterland of a student's school experience. You will also have named safeguarding leads in your school, and there may be other professionals whom you can call upon when you feel out of your depth. In the first analysis, given your first duty as a tutor is to *notice*, if you notice something amiss with your student – a change in behaviour in tutor time, perhaps, a change in punctuality, a student starting to come in looking dirty or dishevelled, sudden changes in weight, changes in social relationships – and feel uncomfortable talking to the student about it, then you should ensure that you flag it up and pass it on. Always use your school's information system to record such interventions and conversations.

Being a tutor can be a wonderful experience and you will probably only really know the impact you have had when either you or your tutee leaves the school, and the student feels the need to tell you. These are poignant, emotional moments.

Which leads me to another piece of advice, which pertains not only to tutoring but to all areas of your teaching career. Hold on to thank you notes, emails of thanks or appreciation, or cards. When you have a really terrible day, use them as therapy. There is nothing as uplifting when you're feeling low as reading about the things you have done which have actually led someone to sit down and take the time and effort to say "thank you".

Student Voice

In his guidance about student engagement and raising the aspirations of young people, Professor Russell Quaglia advocates the extensive and real use of Student Voice when deciding about anything pertaining to a school. The students are arguably the most important stakeholders in a school community and they are the beneficiaries of our product, which is the best education we can deliver.

The degree to which Student Voice is really heard in any school varies widely. Most schools will have a school council, or a school parliament, or a student panel. Engagement with these by either students or the adults in the community varies widely, and no one should underestimate the difficulty of engineering real student engagement at an operational level. The problem is that where the representation of Student Voice has historically been patchy or tokenistic, there is a real resistance to participation among students. It's that old chestnut – why would you give up time and effort to do something which is essentially pointless? The pattern with school councils tends to be that they are full of year 7s, bursting with reforming zeal, and then when nothing happens the enthusiasm ebbs away and in its place comes disillusion, and this pattern continues until everyone gives up and forgets about it.

The good news for teaching professionals is that Student Voice needs to be championed by one passionate, democratic and energetic teaching professional. That person cannot be a senior leader; any student representation which is under the heavy hand of senior management can never thrive. For starters, students will never be as open and honest with a Deputy Head about what they perceive as the strengths and shortcomings of the school as they will be with Mr Edwards from ICT; and second, any member of the SLT will be aware of all that is going on in the school and there will be a temptation for them to knock back any criticisms coming from students with a summary of why it's not a problem or will shortly cease to be a problem.

Student councils or parliament, or whatever names you use, need to be run by students. Ideally, a group of senior students will come together with the encouragement of that one energetic and enthusiastic teacher and decide on form and role. They will recruit students from younger year groups. They will choose a link teacher who will help get them access to the adults in the school to whom they need to talk. They will be given time to meet, and a notice board or virtual notice board where they will display personnel, notices, minutes and calls for help. They will have regular slots to talk to SLT and the board of governors. They will make things happen, and it will be self-perpetuating.

But beware – as in so many areas of a school there must be succession planning. Teachers move on. Students move on even more quickly. Senior students leave en masse. There must be a sense that the next year group of students should prepare to take the lead. The enthusiastic energetic link teacher needs to ensure that they engage other energetic enthusiastic teachers who can take over the leading of the project. At any time the loss of people can cause the breakdown of the project. This happens all the time in schools – they are notoriously bad at succession planning in any area that's not a classroom subject.

More good news for those who want to show they're making a positive contribution to the wider life and ethos of the school, or those who just really want to get stuck into improving their school community, is that there is always, *always*, a need for teachers to step up to the plate when it comes to Student Voice, and there is no better way to understand the wider nature of the school in which you have chosen to teach.

Teaching and Learning Groups

In every school there will be some forum in which teachers come together to discuss pedagogy. How active and strong this is, and how democratic in nature, is probably as good a measure of a staff's morale and mental health as any.

The basic will be a teaching and learning group which is run by a member of senior management and to which every department sends a colleague. The Senior Leader will send out an agenda, drawn up by them according to the needs of the school development plan, which has in turn been drawn up by Senior Leaders with contributions from Heads of Department. The meeting will be led from the front, and attendees will go away with a list of actions which may have already been decided or which may come out of discussions in the group, and then progress against those actions will be measured by the Senior Leadership Team.

Even if your teaching and learning group is run in a way that seems top-down, authoritarian and directive, there is still enormous benefit to be derived from getting involved, receiving useful ideas and input, and making your thoughts, and the thoughts of your department, known. That agenda can be changed, and ideas can be taken on board. The worst case scenario is that T&L meetings are attended by people who were nominated to go, who don't want to be there, and who will be quiet and hope the whole thing is over as quickly as possible. (It's that thing again about people not wanting to do things which will make no difference and are a waste of time, which could be better spent planning lessons or marking.) Hopefully, the people who are there have a genuine interest in pedagogy and want to share knowledge from other departments and take back to their own some great new things to try, or solutions to problems that have dogged them. (I remember covering a lesson in a science classroom and finding a pile of proformas which the teacher would use to set work to be done in a detention – it was brilliant and I picked one and took it back to the department.) These meetings to share ideas are vital in saving departments time by sharing ways of doing things that everyone has to do. As a teacher who wants to make a wider contribution, attending Teaching and Learning meetings and being an active participant is a very positive way to make a difference.

Your school may well have evolved beyond the simple Teaching and Learning group and there may be multiple ways to get involved. If you've come into teaching, then presumably you're interested in developing as a teacher. Participating in teachmeets, lesson study groups, department groups, teaching triads or whatever else is on offer in your school, is a fantastic and democratic way to do this. Most teachers understand that every teacher, from the most junior to the most experienced, has something that all others can learn from, and most schools will afford everyone the opportunity to share their ideas. The more, the better.

Extra-Curricular Activities

Even if you have a huge workload and it feels like a struggle to come up for air and blink into a world beyond teaching, taking part in or leading an extra-curricular club offers something fresh to a teacher's life. If they can find the will or energy to do so.

Extra-curricular activities not only provide opportunities for students to learn other skills and knowledge, but also allow teachers and other members of the community to flourish as individuals with lives beyond their subject, as people with real passions, and to share them with the young people in their care. So a school that boasts teachers leading First Aid sessions, girls' football, and clubs for coding, robotics or stand-up comedy, as well as an attendance officer leading a weekly Zumba class, an LSA gardening with some young students, a couple of parents running a Sewing Bee and the Bursar getting involved in Young Enterprise – all this shows signs of the school being a healthy place where members of staff want to extend their involvement with the students, and where all have a chance to play a fuller part in the life of a real community. It also enables the adults in the community to work together in a more unified, purposeful and democratic way.

Taking part in extra-curricular activities must always be something that is an opportunity, not a duty. Anything that is expected of teachers in addition to the enormous burden, especially on teachers new to the profession, will be intolerable and will have a negative impact on their mental health and staff morale. Any sensible Senior Leadership Team will see the provision of a carefully planned programme of extra-curricular activities as something to be nurtured and developed and to be staffed by volunteers.

Once the programme is devised and launched, it is equally important that schools encourage but do not force students to take part. Many young people already spend a great deal of time outside schools in organised activities, and the school is not always aware of what they do in their after-hours time. There are students who are already busy, and there are students who need time for their internal life, who need to be quiet and alone and untroubled when they leave the hubbub of school life. Taking part in extra-curricular activities should feel like a great world of opportunity which creates a buzz around a school and its community. It should provide breathing space for young people and adults alike; at best it can provide an escape path and an opportunity to shine for those who sometimes find it difficult to be noticed in the course of their everyday education.

Mentoring

It is a wonderful privilege to mentor younger teachers in our profession, and it requires some humility to do it properly. Being chosen as a mentor is not being told that you are there to pass on all the wealth of your wisdom to some ignorant newbie. What you are there to do is to bring out of the younger teachers the best teacher they can become.

This is tricky because you may be called upon to mentor teachers who are not like you, who don't have the same teacher personality and will therefore never teach like you. What you want to do is to observe that person teach and try to see what they are good at. Perhaps it is human nature, but observing anyone do anything with a view to coming up with a judgement tends to mean that you note down every little thing they get wrong, and then only come up with one or two generalised positives when required to give feedback. (It's amazing how many teachers do this to each other, when they would never dream of meting out this sort of treatment to the young people in their classes.) So those who are mentored by an experienced teacher are left in no doubt as to all the myriad ways they could improve, but no real idea of what strengths they have to build upon. This does not enable a colleague to refine their teacher personality.

Strictly Positive Mentoring, looking for what a teacher is doing right, is an incredibly important job. We all know there is a shortage of teachers these days, that more teachers are leaving the profession than are joining it, and that it is widely perceived as a difficult job. And not everyone can teach, it is true. But what we must do as mentors is to help those brave souls who come into our profession to become, from a standing start, the best teacher they can be. And to do that, we employ all the nurturing, positive techniques that we would use when encouraging a student to achieve their potential.

Among the raw ingredients of a good teacher that we should be looking for are:

Rapport
- *an easy manner with a class*
- *a clear liking for young people*
- *the ability to listen*

Behaviour management
- *the ability to "read the room"*
- *the confidence to use silence*

Subject knowledge
- *confidence in knowledge*
- *ability to accept correction*

The ability to correct sensitively
- *being able to react appropriately to wrong answers*
- *guiding students to correct answers*

Presence
- *talking so students will listen*
- *a good balance of talk and silence*

The ability to give instructions
- *clarity and economy of expression*
- *checking that instructions have been understood*

❖ Develop effective professional relationships with colleagues, knowing how and when to draw on advice and specialist support

In many ways teaching is a funny old profession. In one regard, you're the king of your castle with a great deal of freedom to teach your students in your own class in your own classroom (if you're lucky!) with your own methods and your own resources. Once the classroom door is closed it's just you and the students, and you make the rules.

On the other hand, you cannot work alone in the school of today. You are accountable to your colleagues in the department, to your Head of Department, the Senior Leadership Team, the pastoral leaders, and not least to the parents and the students.

It is essential to maintain an appropriate balance between being a self-motivated independent colleague,and adhering to the rules and mores of the institution in which you work, mindful of the needs of all. And that brings us back, once again, to relationships. We have already talked at length about the way to develop positive relationships with the students you teach. Now we need to talk about the relationships you will need to develop with the adults in the community.

Novice Teachers

At the start of a teaching career, all teachers will feel ill-equipped to carry out their duties effectively and will need lots of help from many, many different people. It is to be hoped, as I've said before, that a mentor or mentors will be provided to help the novice navigate the many complex demands of the profession, and regular meetings scheduled to give them space to ask questions or air concerns or talk about the things that went wrong. Hopefully, this assistance and these meetings will be non-judgemental and supportive, allowing the trainee or newly qualified teacher to experiment and find out through trial and error what suits them, who they are as an educator, and what they need to develop towards proficiency and expertise.

A consideration for every novice teacher is how many questions to ask their new, more experienced colleagues. How do you know how and when to draw on specialist advice? I recently reread the interim report given to me after my first placement (kept, like all reports and assessments, for sentimental reasons...) and was struck by the comment that I had "*milked* members of the department for information". I still can't quite work out whether the writer thought that was a good or a bad thing. I hope it was good. Certainly now, as an experienced teacher and mentor, I want the new arrivals to be confident enough to ask lots of questions and seek lots of advice. I worry about those who profess confidence and don't ask for advice – if you think you know it all then you are riding for a fall, whereas if you don't know it all but don't want to show your lack of knowledge, then it's a toss-up between your colleagues and the students as to who will find you out first!

My guidelines as to how and when to ask for support would be something like this:

- *Ask everybody for help*
- *Write down what you're told*
- *Don't try and implement all the advice at once. Prioritise, or ask your mentor to help you prioritise. Make colleagues aware of your priorities*
- *Choose one or two things to work on at a time*
- *Decide how you're going to make progress in those areas*
- *Show that you are working on those one or two things. Really stick at it –make progress and show progress in those one or two areas*
- *Once you have acquired proficiency in one area, find out what else you should be improving and repeat the cycle*

Pitfalls in this cycle, things that drive mentors insane are:

- *Asking for help and not listening to the answers*
- *Asking other colleagues the same questions in the hope that you'll get an answer you like better – we do talk to each other!*

- *Forgetting what you're told and continuing to make the same mistakes over and over again*
- *Saying that you haven't got around to addressing what you identified as the most important thing to tackle with your mentor*
- *Not accepting responsibility. Blaming everything that goes wrong in your lesson on someone else – usually the kids. This disempowers you as a professional – the only behaviour you can change is your own*

A Word About Observations

Observations are a fact of life in modern teaching. You will be observed and you will get the chance to observe. This will happen all your career; as a Head of Department you will still be observed on a regular basis – just not quite as often. Some of it will be developmental; in fact, hopefully a lot of it will be developmental but some will be judgemental. Always remember that observation is probably the most useful tool you have to make yourself a better and better teacher.

When you first get into a job, try and get into as many lessons as possible to observe the kind of teaching that is happening around you. Start off in your own department and see everyone – you will get very direct and immediately useful techniques from them as they are teaching the same material you will be teaching. As soon as you can after that, however, start asking colleagues in other departments if you can come and see their lessons.

You will probably be told about the staff member whose legendary rapport, classroom management, student engagement or whatever other skill makes them someone you really must see. Go and see them and try to gauge what it is that they are or what they do that makes them so skilful in that area. Be aware that teaching is also about personality. Some colleagues are incredibly calm and measured, and don't need to do much jumping around and showboating to teach effectively – they are skilful in using their calm and steady nature to effect a positive classroom environment. Others are more bombastic, with louder voices and a more forceful presence – they use this force to bring about the same end result. See both, but remember that if you are a bombast then you'll probably get more that you can use in your practice from other similarly extravert colleagues, whereas although you will probably admire and wonder at your calmer colleagues, you probably won't be able to use some of what they do; and the same is true in reverse.

Whether or not colleagues will be happy for you to come into their classrooms will tell you a great deal about the morale of the staff. Some may welcome you and be flattered that you want to come into their room and will enjoy your presence. Others may not want you there. Respect colleagues whether or not they accept your request. There will always be reasons for it.

Some schools will have compiled a list of colleagues who have particular skills and who have already agreed to being observed. Some of them may have an open-door policy, which means you can drop in without notice. I would still ask permission – apart from anything else, it's polite. It may not always be convenient or useful to you to observe a lesson either – on occasion I have had PGCE students or NQTs drop into my lessons when students were silently engaged on an assessment. They have wasted their time coming over and sitting in.

Similarly, when you have been allocated a class and upon meeting them have found them tricky or failed to "click" with them, find out who works well with them. LSAs are brilliant for this – following a student around they observe teachers in their daily habit, not just when they know they're going to be observed. They are far more informative in this regard than the SLT with their data who only ever see the polished up, shiny lesson! Ask an LSA which teacher is good with this class and have a word with that colleague or send them a quick email.

I would counsel *all* teachers, at every stage of their professional development, to go and observe others. Anyone who believes that they are perfectly cooked, that they have nothing left to learn from younger colleagues or colleagues younger to the profession, has made the decision to start being irrelevant. But if you're an older or more experienced teacher and you want to go and observe someone new to your school, do make it clear that you are doing so because you think *you* can learn something from *them* – otherwise they might think they've done something wrong and you're there to file another negative report about them.

More Experienced Teachers

It is probably true that you are always learning in every profession, but nowhere is it as startlingly obvious as in teaching.

To begin with, we're working with children, and children and their worlds change with fantastic speed: the way they speak, the way they think, that their beliefs and assumptions can be relied upon to be unreliable over time. It is true that time kaleidoscopes as we grow older, and so it is easier and easier to be lulled into learning some new lingo that has caught on in your school community and then to continue to use it for that tiny bit too long and be met with howls of derision when you say something is "wicked" and are told that no one says that any more. It has always been that way – I can remember the palpable embarrassment, like beetles crawling down my spine, when my Dad referred in front of my friends to something as "cool" when *literally* no one said that any more.

On a more important point, technology moves on, theory moves on, belief systems move on, ethics and morality move on. As we get older it becomes more difficult to keep up, and the more curmudgeonly among us might assure ourselves that we're right – it's the developments which are ridiculous. I would never suggest that we should abandon entirely the ways in which we are used to teaching, but we should be cognisant of new developments in our subject and in pedagogy itself and ensure that we do not simply dismiss it as gimmickry or fashion. As we teach learners we should recognise the value of learning and continue to demonstrate enough humility to regard the professional relationships we have as mutually helpful, learning from our junior colleagues as well as teaching them.

❖ Deploy support staff effectively

There is not nearly enough respect in our schools for our support staff. While in general parents and students understand that a level of respect is due to teaching staff and senior staff who are nearly always accorded courtesy titles of Mr, Mrs, Ms, Dr etc, often there is less explicit politeness afforded the school receptionist, secretary, catering staff, caretakers and others. This is something most schools are working to correct, and is not something we as teachers can do much about, except to hold the line when we observe a lack of respect accorded these colleagues.

In the context of deploying staff, we are here talking about the support staff who have explicit responsibility for students – teaching assistants, learning support assistants, special needs support staff, behaviour management staff and foreign language assistants among them.

There is not nearly enough understanding amongst teachers in many schools of the extraordinary benefit which the learning support assistants, teaching assistants and SEN support staff can bring into a classroom. I would argue that the lack in many schools of a properly constructed programme of professional development for our support professionals is not only a great shame, but means that too often we lose a critical resource from our classrooms. Committed and conscientious colleagues work with our most challenging students, are required to do a job which is mentally and emotionally draining, are paid a pittance and don't see any professional progression, and they leave. The positive effect that these professionals have on the young people to whom they dedicate so much is wildly underestimated and undervalued, and the negative impact of their departure on these students can be catastrophic.

Often you will work in a particular class with a particular member of the support staff – let's call them an LSA – who is charged with supporting a specific student or students. The nature of the business of teaching being as it is, and the demands on our time so often more than we can cope with, what happens generally is that the class comes in and the LSA comes in with them. You nod to the LSA and exchange greetings. You may show them the page of the textbook you're working on or give them a brief summary of the work you're doing in class; often you won't even do that. The LSA either has a seat next to the student, or they stand hovering near the student, leaning on a radiator. They keep an eye on what is happening with the students they are charged to support. You start to teach your lesson. At the point where one of the LSA's charges calls out or acts up in some way, the LSA glides over to them and as discreetly as possible intervenes to steer them back on track. You, relieved that you don't have to break your teaching to manage the behaviour, carry on. At the point where the teaching from the front stops and an exercise or discussion is set, the LSA moves closer to the student or students to facilitate their involvement in the activity. The student in their care is one less to worry too much about and you let them get on with it. At the end of the lesson if things have gone well, you'll express relief to them and if they haven't, you'll have a quick debrief as to what to do now before the next lesson. The LSA rushes off to catch up with their charges before the beginning of their Maths lesson. You'll be grateful they were there, because when they are not, when sickness means that the LSA schedule has to be rejigged and the student turns up alone and unsupported, things don't go nearly as smoothly, and the lesson is often derailed.

The system works, but couldn't it work a great deal better with just a little more organisation and cooperation? We teachers often miss a whole basket of tricks when we operate on this ad hoc basis with LSAs and support staff. We need to understand that whereas we are the holders of the expertise in the subject, they are probably the experts on the individual students, those students who are the ones we probably have to accommodate more in our planning than the majority of the students.

That LSA will see Charlie in every context. He or she will see how she responds to different teachers and teaching styles. They will have learned to be alert when certain activities happen, will know which of the students Charlie is going to chat to in unsupervised moments, and who she's got a beef with this week which might spill over into a violent confrontation. They'll know Charlie was out until 2 am and brought back to the house by the police or that Charlie's granny died last week and she's going to the funeral this afternoon. They'll know she's being bullied mercilessly by a group of "good girls" who are intent on making her understand that she doesn't fit or, conversely, that she's been bullying a kid in the year below. They'll know she's really excited because she's playing in her first hockey match this afternoon, or fearful because she has to go to court to testify in her parents' divorce case. In brief, they have a treasure trove of information and knowledge, all of which could help you interact with Charlie in the most positive way possible.

What neither of you has is much time to discuss Charlie. You, because you're a teacher and are juggling 173 things on your to-do list; and he or she, because no school really ever has enough people to do the job they're doing, and the sickness and attrition rates are high so they often have to multitask and often support students they don't know as well. But each of you can make the other's life easier by a sharing of information.

So how do you exchange essential information in the most economical and effective way?

Some of what you'll want to know will probably be provided by the SENCo to all teachers by way of a digest. This should include learning methods that Charlie finds helpful, stumbling blocks for her, and some strategies for helping her academically or behaviourally, whatever her difficulties are. If you as the teacher are proactive, you can find out extra information from the LSA before you take on the class, on a training day or over coffee one day before school. You can look over the class list so that the LSA can advise you where to seat Charlie to help her, the class and you most effectively. They may warn you about flashpoints in the material which might need sensitive handling – avoid a family tree task in Spanish, because there are significant family difficulties at the moment; think about an English lesson on idiom, because Charlie is very literal and becomes easily confused by abstract ideas – and in turn they may ask you for brief summaries of the lesson before the class enters the room, in order best to support her.

Depending on your subject the LSA may need more or less from you in order to know how to help Charlie in this lesson. Non-linguists may benefit from a vocabulary list; scientists could usefully provide a glossary of terms that have been used in prior study. In fact, you could suggest to your department that such aids be devised for all topics in order to help the LSA to help you. Once you have a way of working with an LSA about a student, it doesn't take much extra work to meet them for a few seconds before you open the door – they brief you on anything about the student that you need to know, and you brief them on anything they need to know about the material and the way you propose to teach it.

In addition, if you observe or hear something about the student which you are worried about or which you feel the need to pass on, do not be afraid to pass it on to the LSA or the SENCo. It may be something they have been too busy to notice, or it may be something that that child has been hiding. Support staff are good at broaching difficult conversations privately and discreetly, never mentioning your name. The worst you can be is wrong, and that's absolutely fine.

❖ Take responsibility for improving teaching through appropriate professional development, responding to advice and feedback from colleagues

There is Career Professional Development, and there is Career Professional Development. In teaching we are lucky in that we have a number of days that are ring-fenced and dedicated to the business of becoming better at our jobs. It's a fabulous thing. Except that it's not always as well-conceived as it should be, and sometimes we feel that it's not particularly useful to us. Now, some humility is necessary when thinking about this because each of us is a cog in the wheel and the training might not be as useful to your cog as it might be to someone else's. Given that it's practically impossible to tailor training 100% personally, we must all accept that a best fit for all is all we can really hope for.

The terminology here is interesting – "take responsibility for improving teaching...". As previously discussed, expertise is not limited to the crania of the senior professionals in a school, and most teachers can probably step up to the plate and deliver some important suggestions which others in the community might benefit from. We can't be responsible for the bought-in CPD which provides insights into some element of our practice which we cannot see when operating at the heart of a single institution. There will always be failings or weaknesses in any school and somewhere, someone – an expert on that subject – will be a useful person to listen to. The responsibility of the classroom teacher in that situation is simply to set aside any cynicism and listen with an open mind and take on the messages.

Aside from that, a sensible senior leader in charge of CPD in these straitened times will look very closely at the skills and gifts of the teachers in their staff and see how they can boost morale at the same time as improving teaching by using their own staff to teach each other to the common good. A skills audit is a good tool to use in a school and is easy to do in a community where teachers know they're trusted and respected. In a school where there is poor morale and leaders and soldiers regard one another with distrust it is not something that could be carried out in a positive way. In a skills audit a school will ask all teachers to identify in which areas they have high skill levels, and to say where they feel they could benefit from some extra assistance. They should be led to understand that they're not holding up their hands and saying they're brilliant or rubbish at anything, just that they are more or less confident. Then the good behaviour managers could run a session for the less confident behaviour managers, and staff members who use group work effectively could suggest some ways in which those who are less confident could improve their practice in this area – all in an atmosphere of mutual trust and well-being.

Teachers are not generally good at holding up their hands and declaring their strengths and, as a group, are more likely to admit areas of weakness. There are exceptions to this, obviously, but this is a general rule. When I moved into teaching from a business role, where most people were very happy indeed to buttonhole you and tell you about all their many and varied gifts, and hardly anybody was apparently less than good at anything, this was one of the many marked differences between the two fields of employment.

There are different ways in which teachers can deliver in-house CPD to one another. In a "teachmeet" scenario, a short time will be set aside and teachers invited to share techniques which they use for a single aspect of their practice, each presenting for no more than five minutes, and teachers making notes on several different ideas which they might like to try on their own classes. Teachmeets are democratic – a PGCE student may bring along a new idea which could be useful to other colleagues, and an experienced teacher will contribute equally. A teachmeet is a powerful and energising tool, and boosts morale by showcasing the breadth of imagination and talent within the community.

CPD carousels are also a great idea. Where a colleague feels they have something to contribute, or senior leaders identify something in their practice which could usefully be shared with the rest of the community, they may organise a day of CPD where there may be six to eight slots and the same material would be presented six to eight times so that all colleagues receive the same messages. Each of these sessions would be 15-20 minutes long and would be presented by one or two teachers. This is an amazingly efficient way of diffusing information throughout the community and has the same morale-boosting effects of a teachmeet.

If you felt you had more to contribute to your colleagues you might like to be a part of an optional programme of twilight CPD sessions which are published ahead of time and where a teacher can go into more detail on some subject they feel passionate about. The snag about twilight sessions is that a) by their nature they take place at the end of the working day; and b) they are optional. In practice this means you can do an awful lot of work to prepare a great session and then find that three people turn up and some of your activities can't be run and the whole thing is slightly embarrassing.

The main thing about you as a teacher and your responsibility for improving teaching is that you as a professional take a hard look at your practice, not just to pick holes in it and beat yourself up about the areas where things sometimes go wrong, but to see what skills you have, and what ideas you have that you're proud of, and to summon up the confidence to claim your skills and your ideas and to want to share them.

Strictly Positive Teaching is about recognising what is going right and using it to grow in your practice and your skill-level and to become a healthier and more confident teacher. Having a Strictly Positive mindset is not just about the way you look at the students – it's about the way you view the whole community and yourself as well. A confident, mentally and emotionally healthy teacher is of far more use to their students than someone who convinces themselves that all that needs examining is the weakness in their practice. By taking care of yourself, you make yourself more able to look after your students.

It's a bit like the instruction when you're taking off in an aircraft that you should put on your own life jacket before attending to children or old people in your care. You can't support others when you're drowning yourself.

❖ Communicate effectively with parents with regard to pupils' achievements and well-being

Communication flow between schools and parents is probably an area where there is enormous divergence between different educational institutions. The most obvious methods of communication are school reports and parents' evenings, when that communication tends to focus on how students have done in the preceding term, and what they need to do to make further progress. Certainly, discussing students' achievements, assuming there have been some (how many of us, searching for a positive have started a report with something like "Sophie arrives at her Physics lessons punctually most of the time..."?) is at the core of both reports and parents' evenings, but there is less often talk about well-being. That is left to the pastoral leaders and then only if there is an absence of well-being. In year 11 most schools, driven by headlines about stress among children in exam classes, will probably take more of an interest in students' well-being.

Many schools ask teachers to communicate with parents when they issue a detention, and teachers duly send a terse little email starting "I regret to inform you that I have had to place Cameron in detention for...". The idea, I suppose, is that when Cameron gets home his mum will give him a talking to about getting it right in school. As Cameron accrues more and more detentions and the emails start coming from middle leaders, the tellings-off become more forceful until mum decides that, frankly, what's the point? So, she deletes the emails as they come in, and Cameron does, or doesn't, attend his detentions, after a while factoring them into his day.

On the other side, there will be some mechanism for applauding kids who get it right. Departments or the Head will send out postcards to applaud Chantelle for doing so well in music, and Chantelle will get a pat on the head and the postcard will go on the fridge door.

It is interesting here that the teachers' standards refer to communicating about students' "achievements and well-being". In other words, they should focus on what is going right for a student in order to work for their mental health. In other words, what we are asked to do as a statutory requirement is to be Strictly Positive.

If you're dreading Cameron's appearance in a lesson and rather hoping that today will be the day he is away, or having a session with the Behaviour Support Manager, or excluded, and he bursts into your classroom and then astonishes you by having a really good lesson with you, making some good contributions and completing all the work in his book, then *notice and acknowledge* your surprise. At the next opportunity, break or lunch or after school, email Mum. Put in the title line "Great lesson in DT for Cameron!" so that she doesn't dismiss it as another detention email and delete it. It doesn't need to be complicated: "Cameron had a great lesson today. He volunteered usefully in class and got all his work done. Please pass on my congratulations." And *send*.

Or, even better, pick up the phone and call Cameron's mum. She will be wary when she hears that you're calling from the school and then delighted when she realises you are calling with positive news. She may even cry on you; she may even cry when she congratulates Cameron when he gets home. She will remember you and Cameron will be grateful. You will feel good, she will feel good, Cameron will feel good.

Whether or not you have the time or inclination to notice one great lesson from a student who is not always conscientious and email or call about it immediately, I would really suggest that you try and create a pattern of sending congratulations.

At the end of the day today, when you're tidying your desk and getting ready to go to the pub, or to football, or home, or whatever your thing is on Friday, or any day, take a moment before logging off your school management system. Look through your registers and find three kids who have properly earned your praise today or earlier in the week. Maybe they volunteered when they usually don't. Maybe they behaved better than normally. Maybe their book was excellent. Maybe they just tried really hard, even though they didn't succeed.

Then pick up the phone and call home (or email, if you don't like the phone). Tell Mum, or Dad, or foster parent, or Granny and ask them to pass on your congratulations. They will be overcome with gratitude, because most of the time they don't get calls with good news. They will make you feel really good and you will leave the premises with a little spring in your step.

And next time the kid arrives in your classroom, you can say conspiratorially, "Did your Mum say I called?" and you will share a very small private smile, and that student will do their very best in the lesson.

Win win. And it takes about a minute.

As I mentioned under Tutoring, it's a good idea to retain all emails you get from parents thanking you for your positive comments and being complimentary about you. Not because I'm suggesting you add them to your files when you apply for promotion (although you can) but because when you're down and you've had a terrible day and doubt your own abilities – and we all have days like that, however long we've been in the profession – reading what amount to testimonials from parents can really lift your spirits and make you feel better about yourself.

Strictly Positive Teaching

CONCLUSION

Last week I was at a birthday party for a friend of my mother's and was introduced to an ex-Head Teacher. The person who introduced us mentioned I was writing a book about teaching, thinking he would be interested.

"So are you just telling people how to teach, then?" he asked, in a slightly challenging way.

Well, no, I explained, what I wanted to do was to suggest ways in which professionals could tweak their existing practice in order to start from a more positive standpoint, in order to create a more positive classroom environment in which teachers could teach and learners could learn more efficiently and constructively.

I hope that is what I've done. To be a Strictly Positive Teacher is to look at all aspects of teaching practice from a positive perspective and to resolve to adhere to the key tenets of the philosophy:

The Seven Rules of Strictly Positive Teaching:

1. *Teachers have positive expectations of learners*
2. *Teachers positively take charge*
3. *Teachers have consistent, fair methods*
4. *Positive effort, behaviour and progress are noticed and rewarded*
5. *Praise is public, specific and leads to reward; negative interaction is private, specific and leads to sanction*
6. *Positives and negatives do not cancel each other out*
7. *Teachers work with students' natures, not against them*

It's taken me a long time to write this. Every so often over the last two years there have been reports in the press of the unrelenting nature of the burden on our young people of academic expectations and societal pressures and each time I have thought that maybe this time measures would be put in place to address these issues, but time and again nothing really happens following the hand-wringing.

School budgets continue to be unbearably stretched and the demands on schools continue to rise and, if anything, the mental health problems in our schools are getting worse.

This month I attended another unbearably sad memorial service for another young person who had succumbed to the strains of modern life. Not enough is said about this tragic waste, and even less is being done. Surely it is up to all of us to do what we can in our life and work to try and help. I believe we, as teachers, can do an enormous amount to make kindness a bigger part of life, and we can do this simply by effecting a few tweaks in our own practice.

The philosophies, techniques and ideas in this book cost little, if anything, to put into practice, and can bring about dramatic change in classrooms. Many professionals will conclude that they already use many of them in their classrooms every day, but I hope that most can find something, if only a tweak in a couple of places, which they can usefully accommodate in their existing practice.

I hope that using at least some of the ideas and techniques of Strictly Positive Teaching will change your teaching, your classroom and your students, and make your professional practice more positive, kinder, healthier and happier!

About the Author

FRANCES COX

Frances Cox has a background in Modern Foreign Languages teaching and pastoral leadership. She has also mentored PGCE students and NQTs, with many of whom she is still in contact. She has recently left school employment to be able to spread the messages of Strictly Positive Teaching, speaking to new colleagues and existing school staffs. She is married with two grown-up children who have taught her almost as much as she has taught them.

For more information or to contact Frances please visit www.strictlypositiveteaching.com.

Printed in Poland
by Amazon Fulfillment
Poland Sp. z o.o., Wrocław